DELICIOUS
MAIN COURSE
DISHES

MARIAN TRACY

DELICIOUS MAIN COURSE DISHES

200 Recipes

DOVER PUBLICATIONS INC.
NEW YORK

Published in Canada by General Publishing
Company, Ltd., 30 Lesmill Road, Don Mills,
Toronto, Ontario.
Published in the United Kingdom by Constable
and Company, Ltd., 10 Orange Street, London
WC2H 7EG.

This Dover edition, first published in 1978, is
an unabridged republication of the work originally
published in 1964 by Charles Scribner's Sons
under the title *200 Main Course Dishes*.

International Standard Book Number:
0-486-23664-1
Library of Congress Catalog Card Number:
78-51492

Manufactured in the United States of America
Dover Publications, Inc.
180 Varick Street
New York, N.Y. 10014

for

CAROLINE and HERBERT FORD

Introduction 🦋🦋🦋

In *The Art of Cookery* by William King, published in London in 1708, he says pithily and pertinently,

"'Tis a sage Question, if the Art of Cooks
Is lodg'd by Nature, or attain'd by Books;
That Man will never frame a noble Treat
Whose whole Dependence lies on some Receit."

It is indeed true and a thinking person may hesitate before adding to the deluge of books on food, some wise and good, some just plain silly and still others a little dishonest in their pretentiousness and inaccuracy. It is because we have so very much choice that it is so difficult sometimes to decide what to have for dinner and in what way we want to prepare it. It is my hope and wish that this book will stimulate you into varying your menus more than people do whatever their economic bracket, to trying dishes unfamiliar to you and to rediscovering some old and neglected favorites. I am currently enjoying the delicate flavor and texture of celeriac or knob celery or celery root. It is called all these names and is hard to come by except in large city markets or pickled in jars at fancy food stores or by growing your own. A young cousin who has grown up in the beef-producing country in Montana has just blissfully discovered the delights of cooking and eating lamb. And I who grew up near what H.L. Mencken called the great protein factory of the Chesapeake, yearn for veal, lovingly and skillfully cooked as it is in New York's excitingly unmelted pot. A Chicago friend long in the South misses pork loins and has trained the Atlanta butchers to cut this elegant pork cut and introduced it to her Southern friends who are familiar with every other way of cooking pork but this. Middle Western friends are beginning timidly to explore the delights of shellfish now available to them in many forms.

It is now possible to enjoy all these foods wherever you live and there need never be a dull meal whether you cook for your family, your friends, or even yourself. We have gloriously abundant and excitingly varied, and safe food. The shelves in our super-markets are piled high with row after row of glowing and sparkling ingredients, from all over the world. They are indeed sights to amaze and enchant visiting kings and queens.

There is no longer any need to break eggs for a soufflé, one by one, into a saucer and to sniff each, lest one bad egg contaminate the rest. Not so long ago, dishes were apt to be either very good or very bad, depending on the 'quality of the ingredients and the skill of the cook.

It is easy to be a good cook in these days of good and varied ingredients, good short-cuts, stoves that register accurately, measuring cups and spoons, electric blenders, beaters, carvers that do most of the tedious kitchen work. It is still difficult to be a superb cook and still possible to be a bad one. To be a truly fine cook one must know and *care* about quality and have the skill in handling the ingredients that comes from experience and a palate.

A palate is not necessarily a gastronomic Geiger-counter which enables you to tell from what hill the grapes were picked to make the wine you drink but something that tells you what olive oil is the finest, how to know and savor the strawberries picked one or two hours before serving, the cheese that is at just the right moment for eating and the eggs truly fresh, and which is the most important to you.

As in the rest of life, there must be some compromise. Presumably, it would be possible to have the best of all food in your own garden and to commute to a large and sophisticated city with tremendous variety and quality, with fresh truffles, fraises de bois and crème fraîche, flown from Paris, and chocolates (surely the best in the civilized world) flown in from Belgium, and so on, but crabs are still best in the Chesapeake and lobsters in Maine. The next best thing is to know how to choose the *best* olive oil, not just a good one; to develop the discrimination of top Pennsylvania Dutch cooks who have the best of all skills and absolute contempt for less than perfect ingredients. In this they cannot be surpassed. It is conceded that the French are the masters of the culinary world. They have learned much from the Italians, who learned from the Chinese and the Greeks, who learned from the Egyptians, and so on, back to the beginning of the Homo sapiens.

I am *not* happy about bread in America which gets worse and worse, but I do not want to become a non-eater like Piero di Cosimo in Vasari's *Lives of the Artists*. Vasari speaks sadly of di Cosimo who was so wound up in his experiments in prospective, so cantankerous and who so hated all mankind that he would not let his apprentices live in, mixed his own gesso, and only ate when he was hungry. And what he ate when he was hungry was a few hard-boiled eggs from a large basket kept near the fireplace. He boiled them "in dozens" said Vasari, while mixing the gesso.

Except for an occasional good bakery and the products of one baking company with country-wide distribution, good bread is obtainable only if you bake it yourself.

Since many people either do not eat dessert or have decided preferences, dessert suggestions have in most cases been omitted from the menus and are given only when desirable for a fully rounded and nutritious meal.

As always, many have tasted and tested and sustained me in many ways, these among others: Caroline Ford, Mary Hamaker, Jean Lapolla, Jean Evans, Horace Coward, Clifford Phillips, Marjorie Newsom, Louise Carter, Elinor Parker, and Leonard Doughty.

CONVERSION TABLES FOR FOREIGN EQUIVALENTS

DRY INGREDIENTS

Ounces	Grams	Grams	Ounces	Pounds	Kilograms	Kilograms	Pounds
1 =	28.35	1 =	0.035	1 =	0.454	1 =	2.205
2	56.70	2	0.07	2	0.91	2	4.41
3	85.05	3	0.11	3	1.36	3	6.61
4	113.40	4	0.14	4	1.81	4	8.82
5	141.75	5	0.18	5	2.27	5	11.02
6	170.10	6	0.21	6	2.72	6	13.23
7	198.45	7	0.25	7	3.18	7	15.43
8	226.80	8	0.28	8	3.63	8	17.64
9	255.15	9	0.32	9	4.08	9	19.84
10	283.50	10	0.35	10	4.54	10	22.05
11	311.85	11	0.39	11	4.99	11	24.26
12	340.20	12	0.42	12	5.44	12	26.46
13	368.55	13	0.46	13	5.90	13	28.67
14	396.90	14	0.49	14	6.35	14	30.87
15	425.25	15	0.53	15	6.81	15	33.08
16	453.60	16	0.57				

LIQUID INGREDIENTS

Liquid Ounces	Milliliters	Milliliters	Liquid Ounces	Quarts	Liters	Liters	Quarts
1 =	29.573	1 =	0.034	1 =	0.946	1 =	1.057
2	59.15	2	0.07	2	1.89	2	2.11
3	88.72	3	0.10	3	2.84	3	3.17
4	118.30	4	0.14	4	3.79	4	4.23
5	147.87	5	0.17	5	4.73	5	5.28
6	177.44	6	0.20	6	5.68	6	6.34
7	207.02	7	0.24	7	6.62	7	7.40
8	236.59	8	0.27	8	7.57	8	8.45
9	266.16	9	0.30	9	8.52	9	9.51
10	295.73	10	0.33	10	9.47	10	10.57

Gallons (American)	Liters	Liters	Gallons (American)
1 =	3.785	1 =	0.264
2	7.57	2	0.53
3	11.36	3	0.79
4	15.14	4	1.06
5	18.93	5	1.32
6	22.71	6	1.59
7	26.50	7	1.85
8	30.28	8	2.11
9	34.07	9	2.38
10	37.86	10	2.74

Contents

Beef and Veal

BEEF POT ROAST

The beef eye of the round is not at all pedestrian when cooked this way. It is a lovely glowing brown and somehow looks more appetizing than pot roasts sometimes do.

1 beef eye round, 4–6 pounds
½ cup olive oil
⅓ cup brandy

1 clove garlic, minced
1 freshly ground black pepper
Salt

Rub the beef with the mixture of olive oil and brandy, and then with the garlic and pepper. Put in a Dutch oven with the rest of the oil and brandy mixture. Put in an oven preheated to 450° for 10–12 minutes. Then reduce the temperature to 350° and cover tightly. It should cook in all about 1½ hours. Add salt just before serving. Serves 4 to 6 or more.

SERVE WITH

Mashed potatoes with a dash of Angostura bitters
Baked scraped halves of parsnips with butter
Wilted dandelion greens—dress with cooked diced bacon, bacon fat, vinegar, salt, pepper, and dry mustard
Rye bread

LONDON BROIL

This is an elegant, easy, and inexpensive way of presenting flank steak the way they do in some of the best chop houses. The potatoes are baked at least an hour ahead of time, according to their age and size, and everything else broiled briefly and quickly, and served immediately. Cut the steak against or across the grain in strips about 1½ inch wide.

Broiled Flank Steak

1 flank steak, 2–3 pounds, neatly trimmed
  Large mushroom caps (at least 2 apiece, preferably more)

Butter
Tomatoes (at least 1 apiece)
Mayonnaise
Finely chopped onion
Salt and pepper

Light the broiler. Wipe off the mushroom caps with a piece of lemon. Remove stems and save for another time. Put a small lump of butter, about ½ teaspoon, in each cap. Cut tomatoes in halves; drain. Mix the mayonnaise with the onion and pile loosely on each cut tomato half. Place the flank steak about 3 inches from the broiler. After 2–3 minutes, add the tomato halves, placing them at the side for ease in turning the steak. After 5 minutes on one side for rare, turn and add the mushrooms. Remove when done (each stove is a little different in its timing), and serve immediately. Serves 4.

SERVE WITH

Baked potatoes
French bread

STEAK AU POIVRE

There are many versions of this around but I am including it because it is one of the best ways of cooking steak and we are a nation of steak eaters. Fish steaks are excellent cooked in the same manner. Peppercorns are cracked for this dish with a potato masher or rolling pin or you can buy the coarsely cracked peppercorns. A pepper grinder does not work because you need a much coarser grind.

4 Delmonico steaks, trimmed of fat
2 tablespoons coarsely cracked black pepper
¼ cup butter
2 tablespoons olive oil
2 tablespoons brandy or whiskey

Press the peppercorns with your hand liberally on both sides of the steaks. Wrap loosely in paper and let stand 3 hours or overnight, so that the flavor permeates the steak. Broil as usual and, if you are using an open broiler, make a sauce of the rest of the ingredients and pour over the steak when serving. If pan-broiling, heat the fat, butter, and olive oil and sear the steaks on both sides and keep hot. Flame with brandy and remove from the pan after cooking either briefly or to the desired doneness. Keep warm, pour the juices from the pan over the steaks, and serve. Serves 4.

SERVE WITH

Scalloped potatoes Provençal (p. 196)
Cucumbers, diced radishes, and spring onions with sour cream
Poppy seed rolls

PAN-FRIED STEAK WITH OYSTERS AND
PURÉE OF MUSHROOMS

This purée of mushrooms is like the distilled essence of mushroom. The French serve it with chicken cooked in cream and wine, or use it as a base for other sauces. I prefer to use it with a meat that doesn't have any cream. The steak on this menu is pan-broiled on either side and then transferred to a hot platter with a lump of butter; then a few oysters, say a half pint, are cooked in the steak juices just until the edges curl. Add a lump of butter if the juices seem insufficient. Put on the platter over and around the steak.

Purée of Mushrooms

2 pounds fresh mushrooms
   Salt and pepper

2 or 3 scrapings of nutmeg
2 cups heavy cream

Chop the mushrooms fine until as smooth as applesauce. They also can be put in an electric blender and the switch flicked on and off several times until they are chopped. Either way they should be put in a fine strainer to drain. Then cook in a saucepan over low heat for ten minutes until all the water is evaporated. Add salt and pepper and cream and cook together 15–20 minutes. Makes about 3 cups.

S E R V E   W I T H

> Steak and oysters
> Barley pilaf (p. 209)

CHINESE BEEF WITH GREEN PEPPERS
AND TOMATOES

This is a stir-fry dish that uses one of the good Chinese cooking techniques. The cooking is very brief and the vegetables end up crisp and savory. The cooking itself takes only a few minutes, the cutting up of the ingredients, which is done ahead of time, sometimes takes more.

1½ pounds beef sirloin or flank steak

2 green peppers, cut strips, seeds and white membrane removed

1 medium-sized onion, sliced

1 clove garlic, minced

1 tablespoon fat

1 tablespoon cornstarch

1 can (No. 2) tomatoes or 4 medium-sized fresh tomatoes, skinned, cut in small pieces and seeds removed

Salt and pepper

Cut the steak lengthwise with the grain, then slice against the grain, and then in strips, very very thin, about ¼ of an inch. Brown the garlic in the fat in a skillet. Add the onions and green peppers to the garlic and fat, and stir until almost tender. Add the sliced beef and stir until half done. Season to taste and add tomatoes. Fresh tomatoes may be used if you wish but, if so, add a teaspoon of sugar to remove tartness. Cook until tender. Mix a little cornstarch with cold water and add for thickening. Serves 4.

SERVE WITH

Rice

Endive leaves with individual bowls of seasoned olive oil for dunking

POT ROAST IN CHINESE MARINADE WITH
VEGETABLES BAKED SEPARATELY

This uses the same basting liquid as that used in the pork chops (p. 74) and the turkey cooked Chinese style (p. 140). The left-over marinade can be re-used within 2 weeks if it has been refrigerated.

1 pot roast, 3–4 pound rump or eye of the round marinade
2 bunches carrots
1 bunch parsnips

1 pound medium-sized yellow onions
Butter
Salt and pepper

Sear the pot roast over a high flame, and put in a Dutch oven with the liquid up to halfway. Cover tightly and cook over a low flame 2–3 hours until the meat is tender and most of the liquid has been absorbed. About 1¼ hours before the roast is done, start baking the vegetables in a 350° oven. The carrots and the parsnips should be scrubbed and lightly scraped (the skin lightly scraped off, but not entirely, which means doing an intentionally sloppy job). Cut in halves or quarters, according to size, and bake on a cooky sheet. Dot the vegetables with butter. The onions are baked whole in their skins, then peeled before serving. Serve the meat on a platter surrounded by the baked vegetables. Serves 4–6.

SERVE WITH

Corn muffins

PLANKED STEAK WITH STUFFED MUSHROOMS AND DUCHESS POTATOES

Why do you serve a steak on a plank? To be different, of course. There is something dull about looking at a meat and two vegetables night after night, no matter how fond you are of them. Vary the presentation as often as you do the food you cook.

1 steak, 1½–2 inches thick (the weight will vary)
¼ cup wine vinegar
¼ cup oil
1 minced clove garlic
Salt and pepper
Mashed potatoes, (the instant kind made with milk and lots of butter, or made from scratch)

2 egg yolks
¼ teaspoon nutmeg
Mushroom caps, stuffed (p. 53)

Marinate the steak in the vinegar, oil, and garlic for an hour or two, or longer. Broil or pan-fry on one side from 5–8 minutes. Season and center on a heated plank, uncooked side up. Mix the warm mashed potatoes with salt, pepper, and the slightly beaten egg yolks. Beat until fluffy. Put through a pastry bag or use a spoon and make a loosely piled border on the plank. Place the mushrooms to be broiled around the steak and inside the potato border. Put under the broiler 2–4 minutes, until the potatoes and the mushrooms are lightly browned. Serve immediately. Serves 4.

SERVE WITH

Cold sliced tomatoes sprinkled with finely chopped parsley and fresh basil, if available
Hot rolls

There are some, not many it is true, who admire the art that goes into concocting a truly fine stew, and prefer it to just another steak. This one, with dumplings, is a long-loved German version.

1½ pounds chuck beef, cut in chunks
1 pound fresh peas or ½ box frozen
1 medium-sized can tomatoes
1 pound onions, peeled

1 bunch carrots, scraped and diced
½ pound turnips, scraped and diced
Salt and pepper

Cook the beef, carrots, onions and tomatoes slowly for about 1 hour. Add the turnips, peas, and some water if necessary, for the usual slightly soupy consistency. Add salt and pepper at this time. Serves 4 to 6.

Dumplings

1 cup flour
1 egg

½ cup milk

Mix and knead the ingredients into dough. Twenty minutes before serving drop by spoonfuls into the stew and cover tightly. Steam for 20 minutes without looking at them.

SERVE WITH

Artichokes Vinaigrette

BEEF STEW II

The vegetables in this recipe are a little different from the conventional stew ingredients and require little preparation time. The seasoning recommended is another short cut.

2 pounds cubed chuck beef
2 tablespoons cooking oil
1 package old-fashioned beef stew seasoning (McCormick's)
10 small white onions
1 can Belgian carrots (small whole ones)

1 cup diced celery, or diced, peeled celeriac, or knob celery
1 package frozen Italian green beans

Sear the beef in the oil in a Dutch oven or stew pan. Add the seasoning and 6 cups of water. Bring to a boil, cover, and reduce heat to simmer. Simmer the meat for one hour and a half. Add the vegetables and cook a half hour more. Thicken gravy if desired. Serves 4.

S E R V E   W I T H

Tomato aspic salad
Hard rolls

BEEF AND PORK GOULASH

A goulash, loosely speaking, is a stew with sour cream as part of the liquid, and seasoned with paprika. The paprika for a goulash should not be the casual supermarket kind that usually has no flavoring. For the flavor of this dish, it is important to search until you find a good one. At Paprikas Weiss in New York, 1546 2nd Avenue, you can buy, as far as I know, the best of all paprikas available in this country. They come in three different "hotnesses," the sweet, half-hot, and the very hot. The very hot is only for the true and very knowledgeable lovers of *hot* paprika. Innocent adventurers have been badly shocked or rather burnt. Many Hungarians prefer the sweet paprika.

2 tablespoons bacon drippings or butter	3 tablespoons flour
1 pound boneless beef stew meat, cubed	¾ cup bouillon
1 pound boneless lean pork, cubed	½ cup Burgundy or Claret wine
1 large onion, minced	1 4-ounce can or ¼ pound mushrooms
2 teaspoons good sweet paprika	Salt and pepper to taste
	1 cup thick sour cream

Heat bacon drippings in a large, heavy skillet or Dutch oven. Add beef, pork, and onion. Sprinkle with paprika. Sauté, stirring frequently, until meat is nicely browned. Sprinkle flour over meat and stir well. Add water, wine, and mushrooms (including liquid). Salt and pepper. Cook, stirring constantly, until gravy boils and thickens. Cover and turn heat down to a simmer, stirring frequently, for about 2 hours, or until meat is very tender. Just before serving, stir in sour cream. Taste and add additional salt and pepper, if necessary. Serve with noodles; the ones sauced with cheese are excellent. Serves 4 generously.

SERVE WITH

Noodles
Water cress, endive, and minced onion salad with French
dressing
French bread

ITALIAN STEAK

A pleasing deviation from the ubiquitous steaks and hamburgers.

1¼ pound top round beef, cut in 1½ inch by 4–5 inch strips	Salt and pepper Garlic, minced Grated Romano cheese

Sprinkle each piece of meat with salt, pepper, minced garlic, and the Romano cheese. Roll up and skewer on toothpicks. Run under the broiler and cook 5 minutes on each side. Serves 4.

SERVE WITH

Ghivech (page 200)
Pepper rolls—brown-and-serve rolls, sprinkled with melted
butter and cracked black pepper before putting in the oven

BOILED BEEF DINNER

In this somewhat traditional beef dinner, serve the broth first in the usual manner. There are two basic schools of boiling beef, though I understand no two Viennese who take their boiled beef seriously can even agree about what piece of beef to boil. One of the two main schools cooks the beef in water, so that you get a heavenly bouillon, though less flavor is left in the beef, and the other cooks the beef in bouillon, each giving something to the other.

1 piece bottom round beef, 3–4 pounds, tied for a pot roast
1 bunch carrots, peeled and cut in 2-inch pieces
½ cup finely chopped parsley
1 bunch leeks, split, quartered, washed, and cut in 2-inch pieces
Salt and pepper

Sear the beef on both sides in a Dutch oven over high heat. Add the carrots, parsley, leeks, and water almost to cover the meat. Cover the pot and simmer 2–3 hours over low heat. Season in the last 5 minutes before serving. Serve the broth separately, and the beef sliced on a platter surrounded by the vegetables. Have lots of French bread for mopping up the juice. Serves 4 to 6 amply.

SERVE WITH

Avocado mousse filled with grapefruit segments and pineapple chunks (p. 207)
French bread with sweet butter

SOUP WITH TINY MEAT BALLS

This soup of Italian derivation takes little more time to make from scratch than to heat a canned soup.

Meat Balls

½ pound lean chopped beef   Salt and pepper
1 egg

Soup

3 carrots, scraped and chopped   1 bunch parsley, chopped
3 onions, diced, or   2 potatoes, peeled and diced
3 leeks, well washed and cut   Salt and 7–8 peppercorns
   into 2-inch pieces   3 tablespoons canned tomatoes

Mix meat with egg and seasoning and shape into tiny balls about the size of a radish. Simmer the vegetables together in a pan with 6 cups water for 45 minutes to an hour, or cook under pressure with only 4 cups water in a pressure cooker for 2 minutes and reduce pressure immediately. If cooking the old-fashioned way, cook the meat balls a few at a time in the liquid for about 3 minutes. Remove and start another batch. If cooking under pressure, uncover after reducing the pressure and cook over low heat the same way. When the meat balls are done, transfer to warmed soup plates. Each plate should have 4–5 meat balls. Add the canned tomatoes to the soup and pour into the plates. Serves 4.

SERVE WITH

    Tossed salad
    Club rolls
    Strawberry cheesecake

SIAMESE CURRY

In Thailand curry is used in the Asian way, with handfuls of this and that seasoning tossed into the food cooking, as the mood moves the cook. It is somewhat startling to see seasonings measured by part of a cup rather than by teaspoons and tablespoons, but the curries always taste well and sometimes better after reheating, so that this quantity for 8 could better serve 4 people for two days.

2–4 pounds cubed beef and pork (a little more beef than pork)
3–4 onions, chopped
3–4 cloves garlic, minced
⅓ cup cooking oil or fat from the meat
⅓ cup coriander seeds
⅓ cup ground cumin
2–3 bouillon cubes

⅔ can evaporated milk
1 tablespoon anchovy paste (this is a satisfactory substitute for the fermented fish paste used in Thailand)
Grated rind of ½ lemon
2–3 cups milk or dry skimmed milk, diluted
3½ ounces grated coconut
⅓ cup chopped mint leaves

Sear the beef and pork in a skillet, then transfer to another container. Sauté onion and garlic in the cooking oil or fat from the meat. There should be enough to cover the bottom of the skillet. Rub the coriander and cumin between your palms, letting the heat of your hands warm it a bit. Add it to the onions and garlic and cook a bit in the fat. Add the bouillon cubes and the canned milk, anchovy paste, lemon rind, and black and red pepper. Let it simmer awhile, adding the milk as it starts to dry out. Add the beef and pork cubes and coconut and cook for 1–2 hours, or more. About ½ or ¾ hour before serving, add the mint leaves. Serves 4 for two meals.

SERVE WITH

Rice (1 cup raw rice equals 3 cups cooked rice)
Fresh, frozen, or canned toasted grated coconut
Chopped peanuts
French fried onion rings

Diced fried bananas
Sweet and sour cucumbers (diced cucumbers soaked in sweetened vinegar)
Chutney or, more frugally, watermelon pickle

SAUTÉED BEEF HEART

Many Americans are reluctant when it comes to experimenting with what we squeamishly call "variety meats." All are delectable and nourishing, and usually inexpensive. Most of them, like the sliced beef heart, need only brief cooking, and your butcher, if you have one, will slice this for you. Somehow his knives are always sharper than the ones at home. The texture is excitingly different from more routine meats.

2–3 beef hearts, sliced (depending on size)
3 tablespoons bacon fat or a mixture of butter and oil

½ cup red wine
1 tablespoon finely chopped parsley
Salt and pepper

Sauté the heart in the fat until almost tender. Add the wine, parsley, salt and pepper. Simmer a few minutes more. In all, the cooking time should be around 15–20 minutes, depending, of course, upon the heat and the metabolism of your stove. Serves 4.

SERVE WITH

Mashed potatoes
Slivered green beans and almonds
Hot cloverleaf rolls
Pound cake with custard sauce and Bing cherries

COTTAGE PIE

This is an English way of presenting chopped beef with whatever odds and ends of cooked vegetables happen to be around. There is no reason, of course, why you cannot start with fresh. I find instant mashed potatoes, prepared with milk and butter, quite satisfactory, but those who prefer to mash their own may do so.

4 cups mashed potatoes
3 medium-sized onions, diced
3 tablespoons butter
  Cooked vegetables (peas, carrots, beans, etc.)

1 pound chopped beef
½ can beef gravy
2 tablespoons Burgundy (not the English sort of thing, but good)

Butter an earthenware pie dish and line the bottom and sides with slightly more than half of the mashed potatoes. Sauté the chopped onion in butter and spread on the mashed potatoes. Strew the cooked vegetables on top of the onion. Sauté the beef briefly and add gravy and wine to meat. Put on top of vegetables. Top with the rest of the mashed potatoes. Groove the top of the mashed potatoes one way and then criss-cross at 2-inch intervals with the tines of a fork. Bake in a medium oven (350°) about 30 minutes or until brown. Serves 4.

SERVE WITH

Wilted lettuce salad
Poppy seed rolls

. in vain for the check points of suet and cumin that
This version is not traditional, but good eating just

The purist w·
mark a tr·
the sa·

rbanzo beans
rbanzo beans,

y red beans or
kidney beans,

: pork, scored
round steak
. and chopped
nion, coarsely sliced

1 large can Italian plum tomatoes and juice
1 small can Italian tomato paste
1 large green pepper, seeds and
  core removed and coarsely
  sliced
4 stalks celery and leaves,
  coarsely sliced
6 small hot red Spanish peppers,
  broken

ak dry beans overnight in water to cover. Next day place in deep
pot on top of stove in water they have soaked in, adding more if necessary to cover. Add pork, onion, green pepper, and celery. Bring to a
boil, sprinkle with broken red peppers, then turn heat down to a simmer and cook very slowly for 8–9 hours, stirring occasionally. For the
last three hours, add tomatoes and juice, tomato paste, and the round
steak which has been browned first. Add salt and pepper to taste.
Serves 4 amply. (If the canned garbanzo and red beans are used, 3–4
hours is sufficient.)

SERVE WITH

Cole slaw (p. 83)
Corn bread

SARMA

It may seem like "much of a muchness" to layer
rolls with sauerkraut as they do in Hungary, Yugosl.
and probably some of the other Balkan countries w.
tronomic divisions do not always follow the map-maker
blandness of the cabbage and the tanginess of the saue,
trast well in flavor. Sauerkraut with its acidity muted by s°
has quite a different flavor from that which you get with
and that most Americans don't really like.

1 pound beef ½ pound pork (or 　2 pork chops, 　bone removed) ⎫ ground together twice	16 cabbage leaves, dropp 　　boiling water to so 　　Hungarian sweet papril 　2 pounds sauerkraut, rinse 　　and squeezed dry
1 onion, chopped 3 tablespoons oil 1 egg ½ cup cream 1½ cups rice, cooked 　in milk	Salt and pepper 1½ pounds spareribs (nice, but 　　not obligatory) 1 cup milk

Drop the cabbage leaves in boiling water briefly. Sauté the meat and
onion briefly in the oil. Mix with the egg, cream, and rice. Put a tablespoon of the meat and rice mixture on each cabbage leaf. Roll up.
Arrange 1 layer of cabbage rolls in a casserole that will take top-of-
the-stove heat, then a layer of the rinsed sauerkraut and another layer
of cabbage rolls. Cover with the remaining kraut and the spareribs, if
being used. Add 1 cup milk, cover, and simmer over low heat for 2
hours, adding more liquid (either water or milk) if necessary. Most
of the liquid should be absorbed. Lift the spareribs and stir the sour
cream just before serving. Serves 4 to 6. This is a dish that is better
sometimes the second day, or even the eighth. If you want to use it
another day, naturally you will double or triple the proportions.

* Only the imported adds flavor. The domestic only adds color.

Cottage cheese with hard-cooked eggs and red caviar
Rye rolls

PICADILLO

This is a Mexican meat sauce that is served with black beans and rice.

1½ pounds lean beef, ground
2 tablespoons raisins
½ cup chopped or slivered almonds
1 large onion, chopped
1 can (#2) tomatoes
Salt and pepper

1 teaspoon crumbled dried hot chili
1 clove garlic, minced
1½ cups rice (cooked in 3 cups chicken broth)
1 cup black beans

Cook the meat in a saucepan with ¼ cup water and cook until the water is absorbed and meat browns. Add raisins, almonds, onion, tomatoes, salt and pepper, and the dried hot chili. Serve sauce in a separate bowl to accompany the beans and rice. Serves 4.

Rice, cooked in the chicken broth
Black beans (which have been soaked overnight and simmered with a ham hock)

PASTEL DE CHOCLO

This Chilean corn and meat pie can be very, very elaborate or relatively simple and frugal, as in this version.

2 hard-cooked eggs
2 medium-sized onions, chopped
2 tablespoons fat, preferably bacon drippings
2–3 cups diced, cooked beef, lamb, chicken, or a combination
1 cup bouillon or chicken broth
½ cup seedless raisins
1 teaspoon cumin seed
1 teaspoon oregano or marjoram

Salt and pepper
20 pitted olives, green, ripe, or stuffed with pimientos
1 package frozen corn niblets or 1 can cream-style corn
2 beaten eggs
½ cup milk (1 cup if frozen corn is used)
2 tablespoons sugar
1 tablespoon flour

Sauté the onions in the fat and add the beef, lamb, or chicken, and bouillon, raisins, and seasoning. Simmer ½ hour. Stir the mixture, which should be somewhat the consistency of mincemeat. Put this mixture in a baking dish and scatter over it the olives and the hard-cooked eggs, sliced thin. Beat the eggs and milk and add the sugar, flour, salt, pepper, and corn. Pour over the meat and bake in a medium oven 350° for half an hour, until nicely browned. Serves 4.

SERVE WITH

Paraguayan corn bread—corn bread mix with 1 cup coarsely diced onions and 1 cup grated cheese baked according to directions

CHILI WITH RED BEANS AND RICE

When I was young and wrote my first cook book, never having known a Texan, I worked out a recipe for chili which had the beef in cubes rather than ground, and I still prefer it that way. Since then many Texans have given me recipes for "absolutely authentic" chili using ground beef. The red beans, traditionally served on the side, not in the chili, are often cooked with rice. This decorative version of a rice ring with chili beans in the center is derived from a recipe in Thomas Jefferson's cook book and is not Texan at all.

2½ pounds round steak or chuck, cut in 1½-inch cubes
¼ cup fat from steak, chopped
2 tablespoons olive oil
2 cloves garlic, chopped
3 spring onions, tops and bottoms, chopped

2 cups or more beef bouillon
¼ cup, more or less, good chili powder
1 teaspoon cumin or comino powder
Salt and freshly ground black pepper

Brown the meat and fat from the steak in the olive oil, add the onions and garlic, sprinkle with seasonings, and add the beef bouillon. Bring the mixture to a boil, cover, turn the heat down low, and simmer for several hours. The exact amount of time doesn't matter. It may be done the day before and allowed to "ripen" in the refrigerator or frozen. If it is frozen, the seasonings must be checked on reheating and some fresh chili powder and freshly chopped onion added before reheating. Serves 8.

SERVE WITH

A ring mold of rice cooked in chicken broth and the center filled with canned kidney beans which have been heated with ¼ pound diced scalded salt pork, pepper, and 1 teaspoon oregano. Drain before adding to the ring mold of rice.
Sliced avocado and grapefruit salad
French bread

BAKED MEAT IN A LOAF OR A RING

Too many meat balls and too many meat loaves lose their identity in the ubiquitous tomato sauce. Understand, there is nothing wrong with tomato sauce. It's just that too much and too often gets monotonous and there is a temptation to glare at it and say "get lost." The meat seems more unusual when it is baked in a ring mold. It's true that if some is to be used in sandwiches the loaf shape is more practical.

1½ pounds lean beef, ground
4 slices bread, soaked in ½ cup milk and squeezed dry
⅓ cup freshly grated Parmesan cheese
⅓ cup finely chopped parsley
1 jar (4 ounce) whole pimientos, cut in ½-inch squares

1 teaspoon grated orange peel
1 teaspoon oregano
1 teaspoon Worcestershire sauce
2 teaspoons salt, or according to taste
2 whole eggs

Mix all the ingredients together, and pat into a greased, 5-cup ring mold or Mexican pottery rectangular baking dish. Bake in a 350° oven about an hour. Serves 4 to 6 generously.

SERVE WITH

Mashed potatoes
Sour cream and mushroom sauce—let chopped raw mushrooms stand in sour cream for several hours and then warm very slightly just before serving
Sliced raw radishes with unsalted butter and French bread
Rhubarb Betty (rhubarb baked in layers with buttered crumbs and brown sugar)

CABBAGE ROLLS IN LEMON SAUCE

Most of the European countries roll bits of this and that mixed with rice in cabbage, but there the similarity ends. This Greek version has a delicate and delectable sauce.

1 medium-sized head cabbage	Salt, pepper, oregano
1 pound ground beef	2 eggs, slightly beaten
2 onions, chopped	Juice of 1 medium-sized
1 cup uncooked washed rice	lemon or 2 small ones

Pull the leaves of cabbage apart and drop in boiling water for just 1 minute, to make them pliable. Mix ground beef with onions and the raw rice, salt, pepper, and oregano. Put a spoonful on each leaf or as many as you want to use. Roll up, tucking in the ends, and arrange in a medium-sized casserole, in layers if necessary. Cover with water and bake in 350° oven or cook on top of stove over low heat for 30 minutes. Remove lid and drain cabbage rolls, reserving the liquid. Put the slightly beaten eggs and lemon juice in a small saucepan. Cook over low heat, adding a little liquid from the cabbage until the sauce is smooth and thickened. Pour over the cabbage rolls and serve. Serves 4.

SERVE WITH

Dilled carrot sticks (bought)
Hard rolls

MEAT BALLS IN SOUR CREAM

Meat balls differ from the usual all-beef hamburgers in that they can contain veal and pork and are usually cooked and served in a sauce.

2 medium-sized onions, chopped	Salt and pepper
4 tablespoons butter	1 teaspoon sugar
1 pound chopped beef	1 egg
½ pound mushrooms, sliced	Flour
2 slices dry bread	1 cup sour cream

Sauté the onions in 1 tablespoon butter, until lightly browned. Remove and mix with the meat. In the same pan, sauté the mushrooms in a little more butter for 3–5 minutes, stirring. Remove from the fire. Soak the dry bread in water and squeeze out. Mix the onions, meat, and soaked bread. Add salt, pepper, sugar, and egg, and mix. Shape into about 12 meat balls and dust lightly in the flour. Brown in more butter on each side. Add the sour cream and mushrooms and cook slowly for about 30 minutes. Serves 4.

SERVE WITH

Noodles

Tomatoes stuffed with diced hard-cooked eggs mixed with slightly softened cream cheese (2 eggs to 3-ounce package cream cheese and less than 1 tablespoon of milk)

PASTICHIO

This is a good day-in and day-out dish which is a mish-mash of meat, macaroni, and eggs that is baked until half crusty and half custardy. There are, as in most dishes of this type, many versions.

1 small onion, chopped
⅛ pound butter (½ stick)
1 pound ground beef (lean)
Salt and pepper
½ small can Italian plum tomatoes

½ pound elbow macaroni or noodles or ditalini
3 eggs
1 pint or more milk
1 cup grated Parmesan cheese, or more

Cook the noodles, macaroni, or ditalini in a large pot of boiling salted water until barely tender, then drain. Brown the onion in part of the butter, add ground beef, salt, and pepper, brown briefly, and add tomatoes. Beat the eggs, add the milk and the cheese. Put the drained noodles in a shallow casserole or ceramic pie plate, pour in the egg and cheese mixture. Bake in a medium oven, 350°, 20 minutes to half an hour. Serves 4.

SERVE WITH

Chicory, sliced cucumbers and radishes with French dressing
French bread

QUICK BEEF AND VEGETABLE SOUP

A strong meat broth, rich with vegetables is not only quick and easy to prepare but is soothing and satisfying.

1 pound lean ground beef
1 large can V-8 juice (1 quart, 14 ounces)
2 medium-sized potatoes, peeled and diced

4 medium onions, peeled and quartered
1 large package frozen mixed vegetables
½ teaspoon sugar
    Salt and pepper

Put the ground beef in a dry skillet over medium heat and turn it around in the pan with a wooden spoon until it turns color or loses that raw look. Put in a soup pot, not aluminum, with the V-8 juice and the frozen vegetables, potatoes, onions, sugar, salt, and pepper. Cook until the vegetables are barely done. Check the seasoning, adding more if desired. Serve in large warm soup bowls. Serves 4 to 6.

Cucumber Aspic

4 cups diced cucumbers, puréed
2 cups chicken stock
2 tablespoons grated onions
⅓ cup lemon juice

2 tablespoons unflavored gelatin salt
½ small can water chestnuts, sliced thin
⅓ cup finely chopped parsley
    water cress

Put half the cucumber and half the chicken stock in the container of the electric blender and blend. Pour into a pan and blend the other half and add to the first or put through a food mill. Heat until boiling. Remove from fire. Add the gelatin which has been soaking in the lemon juice. Add seasoning. Stir until dissolved. Put into a 5 cup mold and chill until about the thickness of unbeaten egg white. Remove from the refrigerator, add the water chestnuts and parsley and chill until firm. Unmold and serve on a bed of water cress. Serves 4 to 6.

SERVE WITH

Cucumber aspic
Hot rolls

BIKSEMAD

The Danes prepare food, often just the same old food, in a way especially pleasing to the eye and the palate. Their hash, for instance, tastes very, very good and is decorative, too. The only thing that is different is the diced new potatoes and the catsup and the dill pickle.

1 small onion, chopped
3 tablespoons butter
1½ cups diced cooked meat, beef, lamb, or pork

2 cups diced, cooked new potatoes
½ cup catsup
1 finely chopped dill pickle, preferably kosher

Sauté the onion in the fat, add the meat and potatoes. Brown slightly, stirring well for an even color. Stir in the catsup and heat thoroughly. Just before serving, sprinkle the top with the chopped dill pickle. Serves 4.

SERVE WITH

Italian salad (what the Danes but not the Italians call cooked, mixed vegetables served cold with mayonnaise)
Pumpernickel bread

"21" HAMBURGERS

It is not easy and sometimes impossible to duplicate a dish exactly as it is served in fine restaurants, even when you know the ingredients and cooking procedure. Their ingredients are often of a quality not available in supermarkets and years of skill cannot be matched by a beginner. However, if a little finely chopped celery is added to some freshly chopped beef of an extra fine quality it will taste good although perhaps not exactly like those at "21" in New York.

1½ pounds of freshly chopped, top round steak
Salt and pepper
Celery, finely chopped

⅓ cup butter
1 tablespoon lemon juice
1 teaspoon Worcestershire sauce

Mix the chopped beef, the salt and pepper, and the finely chopped celery. Divide into four oval thick patties. Broil according to taste and serve with a sauce made by heating the butter, lemon juice, and Worcestershire sauce together. Pour over the hamburgers. Serves 4.

Mashed Potatoes with Purée of Celery Root or Celeriac

2 larger celery roots (or celeriac), peeled and diced
3 medium potatoes, peeled and diced

2 tablespoons butter
⅓ cup or more milk or half and half
Salt and pepper

Cook the celery root and the potatoes, separately, until barely tender but not mushy. Put the celery root in the electric blender and blend until smooth or put through a food mill. Mash the potatoes or put through a ricer (potatoes get the wrong texture in a blender). Mix together with the butter, milk, salt and pepper until smooth. Add more milk or butter for a consistency like plain mashed potatoes. Serves 4 to 6.

SERVE WITH

SERVE WITH

Mashed potatoes with purée of celery root (p. 40)
Cherry tomatoes
Poppy seed rolls

TERIYAKI

This is one of the comparatively new and popular ways in which our country is consuming beef at the rate of 150 pounds per person per year. The other meats trail way, way behind.

2 pounds sirloin tip, no fat, cut into strips ⅓ inch thick and 2–3 inches long
1 cup soya sauce
½ cup water

3 tablespoons sugar
3 cloves garlic, minced
1–2 pieces fresh ginger root, minced fine
2–3 tablespoons Bourbon

Make a marinade of all the ingredients and soak the slices of meat for about 2 hours. Thread on bamboo skewers that have been soaked in water first so that they will not catch on fire. Broil briefly. Serves 4.

SERVE WITH

Lettuce stuffed with rice and almonds (p. 208)

ROSEMARY'S BEEF BURGUNDY

This is not the classic version, but one which can be used on a low-cholesterol diet. There is no fat except what is in the meat and in the soup.

3–4 pounds boneless beef chuck, cubed
Flour, salt and pepper
1 can Ancora turtle soup
2 cans Burgundy (use turtle soup can as a measure)
1 clove garlic

1 bay leaf
1 medium-sized onion, chopped
1 chopped carrot
1 small bunch parsley, finely chopped
1 stalk celery, chopped

Shake the cubes of beef, a few at a time, in a bag with flour, salt and pepper. Sear in the bottom of a Dutch oven, using no fat. Add the soup, wine, onion, garlic, carrot, parsley, celery, and bay leaf. Simmer 2–3 hours by which time the meat should be tender and the liquid reduced and thickened. The gravy should need no other thickening. Remove the celery, bay leaf, and parsley, and discard. Serves 6 to 8.

SERVE WITH

Tossed green salad
Garlic bread

CHIPPED BEEF CASSEROLE

Here is an imaginative way of using chipped beef, generally either just creamed or scrambled with eggs.

3 tablespoons butter	1 egg
¼ cup sifted flour	1 cup grated cheddar cheese
1¼ cups milk	3 cups cooked rice (1 cup raw
⅓ cup white wine (dry)	rice cooked in beef or chicken
3 hard-cooked eggs, sliced	broth)
1 cup shredded dried beef	2 tablespoons melted butter

Melt 3 tablespoons butter and blend in flour. Add milk, stirring constantly until it thickens. Add wine and blend. Add shredded beef and sliced hard-cooked eggs to sauce. Beat egg lightly and combine with rice and ¾ cup of the cheese. Line shallow baking dish with about ⅔ of the rice mixture. Spoon on the creamed eggs and beef. Top with remaining rice, sprinkle with remaining cheese, and drizzle with remaining 2 tablespoons melted butter. Bake in moderate oven (350°) about 15 minutes. Serves 4.

SERVE WITH

Diced tomatoes, onions, radishes and cucumbers with sour cream
Hot corn muffins

EMPANADAS

This is a Chilean version of a Cornish pastie but, except for being baked meat-filled circles of pastry, there is very little resemblance. Although the filling for the empanadas is rather rich and filling, they are often served south of the border with coffee as a light snack.

1 pound lean beef, ground	⅓ cup piñons (when not available, use chopped walnuts)
¼ pound fresh pork, ground	
⅓ cup seedless raisins	pie dough enough for top and bottom crust (a ready-mix may be used)
Cinnamon	
Cloves	
Nutmeg	1 egg yolk, diluted with water

Sauté the beef and pork in the fat that melts from the pork for 15–20 minutes. Add the rest of the ingredients and cook 5–10 minutes more. Roll out the pie dough and cut into 6-inch circles (about the size of a bread and butter plate). Put a tablespoon of the mixture in the center of each circle, and fold over into a semi-circle. Mark the edges and press together with the tines of a fork about ½ inch around the edge. Prick a few holes in the top of each one with the fork so that the steam can escape. For an extra professional touch, brush the tops of each with an egg yolk diluted with a little water. Place on ungreased baking sheet and bake in oven pre-heated to 400° for about 15 minutes or until brown. These are served both hot and cold, and sometimes deep-fried until crunchy like doughnuts.

SERVE WITH

Mixed greens with French dressing

BEEF TONGUE WITH HAM SAUCE

A festive and somewhat extravagant way of serving a savory but usually non-festive meat. Tongue is, however, an economical buy as there is no waste and it isn't as large as a ham, which sometimes seems to go on forever.

1 cooked fresh or smoked tongue
½ pound round steak, cut in match-stick pieces
¼ pound cooked ham, cut in match-stick pieces
2 tablespoons butter or, preferably, bacon drippings

2 small onions, chopped
1 bay leaf
1 cup red wine
⅓ cup pistachios or slivered almonds (nice but not obligatory)

Brown the beef and ham in the fat. Add the onions and cook until pale yellow and wilted but not browned. Add the bay leaf, red wine, and ½ cup water. Simmer for about an hour, or until the liquid has been somewhat reduced. Meanwhile, you have skinned and sliced the tongue and arranged it on a platter in a warm place. Pour the sauce over all and serve.

SERVE WITH

Corn pudding (p. 202)
Lima beans
Salad—romaine, grapefruit segments, and French dressing
Hot rolls

OXTAIL STEW

There are so many lovely odds and ends of meat which we tend to ignore, such as oxtail. It makes one of the best of all stews. It is bought disjointed, either by the tail or by the pound, depending upon the region in which you live and the butcher you patronize. It is more robust when made with a head of cabbage, more delicate and unusual and in keeping with European ways of cooking when celery root or celeriac is used, a delicate root-relative of our stalk celery. When that is not obtainable, fresh diced celery stalks may be used but the texture is quite different.

1 or 2 oxtails, cut at the joint, or about 3 pounds
1 cup Burgundy
4 onions, cut and quartered
1 lemon, sliced thin with seeds removed
1 bay leaf, crumbled
Flour for dusting
4 slices bacon, diced
2 fat cloves garlic, cut in half
3 cups bouillon, beef

4 carrots, peeled and quartered
2 cups diced peeled celery root or 1 cup diced celery stalks
8 whole peppercorns
1 teaspoon anchovy paste
2 leeks, well washed and quartered and cut in 2-inch pieces
½ cup dried mushrooms
Large bunch parsley, chopped

Marinate the oxtail, preferably overnight but at least for several hours, in wine, onion, lemon, and bay leaf. Sauté the bacon slowly and drain the pieces on a paper towel. Remove the pieces of oxtail from the marinade and dust with flour. Sauté the pieces of oxtail with the garlic in the bacon fat and transfer to a Dutch oven or an enamelware deep casserole. Add the marinade and bouillon, cover, and bake for 2 hours in 350° oven. Add the vegetables and bake for 1 hour more. Before serving, crumble bacon on top. Serves 4.

SERVE WITH

Cold boiled artichokes with heavily salted olive oil for dipping
Italian bread

TONGUE SALAD WITH SKORDALIA

It does not occur to many what a culinary blessing a cooked tongue in the larder is. It fits so well into so many dishes. It makes, for instance, a very good cold meat salad, especially when dressed with the Greek garlic mayonnaise which contains, in addition to the usual mayonnaise ingredients, ground almonds or walnuts, and, of course, garlic. The extra ingredients may be stirred into a ready-made version of mayonnaise, but the whole mixture can be made more delectably in seconds in your electric blender.

Diced cooked tongue	Skordalia
Diced hard-cooked eggs	Greens
½ small can water chestnuts, sliced and slivered	

Toss together with enough skordalia to hold together. Chill and serve on greens.

Skordalia

1 egg	½ cup blanched almonds or, less traditionally, walnuts
½ teaspoon dry mustard	
1 teaspoon salt	⅓ cup parsley
2 tablespoons vinegar or lemon juice	1 cup salad oil, preferably olive or at least part olive oil
3 cloves garlic	

Put all the ingredients in the blender except the oil. Add a quarter cup of that, cover and turn motor on at low speed. Blend briefly, then uncover and pour in the remaining oil in a steady stream into the center of the whirlpool. Remove and use. Makes 1½ cups.

SERVE WITH

French bread

TONGUE WITH POTATO SALAD

A fresh or smoked tongue cooked in water with a tablespoon or two of mixed pickling spice until the bones at the root wiggle loose is a good food to have on the ready in the refrigerator or freezer.

Potato Salad

1 package pre-cooked frying potatoes or 3 cups boiled diced potatoes
Chicken bouillon or broth
⅓ of the seasoning in package of potatoes if used or salt, pepper and ¼ teaspoon thyme

Warm French dressing (3 parts oil to 1 part vinegar)
⅓ cup chopped spring onions
¼ cup chopped celery
½ cup diced peeled cucumber
Mayonnaise and greens

Cook the frying potatoes according to the directions on the package in the chicken broth with ⅓ of the seasoning that comes in the potato package. Drain and pour on the warm French dressing. Mix with the spring onions and the cucumber, and chill. Just before serving, mix with mayonnaise and place on greens. Surround with sliced tongue. For a still heartier version, surround with sliced pickled beets and sliced hard-cooked eggs and sprinkle with some crisp cooked bacon. Serves 4 to 6.

SERVE WITH

Hot biscuits

STEAK AND KIDNEY AND MUSHROOM PIE

This is a steak and kidney pie as served in England, but not the classic one which is more of a pudding and does not include mushrooms.

1½ pounds round steak, cut in inch- or 1½-inch cubes
1 beef kidney, cut in pieces
4 tablespoons (½ stick) butter
½ pound fresh mushrooms, sliced (if they are not available, use European dried ones, which have more flavor than canned mushrooms)
1 can beef gravy
2 tablespoons red wine
Pastry for a top (use a ready-mix, or regular pie-dough recipe for 1 crust)

Sauté the steak and kidney briefly in the butter, then add the mushrooms. Remove from the fire, mix with the gravy and red wine, and put in a pottery or enamel baking dish, round and shallow. Top with pastry. Bake in a 350° oven 25–30 minutes. Serves 4.

SERVE WITH

> Make-it-yourself fruit salad—have a platter with mounds of mixed melon balls, Bartlett pears, seedless grapes, fresh or frozen whole strawberries or raspberries, orange and grapefruit sections with several dressings to choose from
> Biscuits

KIDNEY STEW

Not all English food deserves the pejorative adjectives usually applied. Their marmalades and jams are wonderful. They have fine baked foods, many excellent cheeses. They know how to cook in good and varied ways many meats that we label squeamishly, "variety meats," and tend to avoid. Although they call them offal, an awful-sounding word to us, for the most part they seem to love them and so do I.

2	beef kidneys or 3 veal kidneys, cut in pieces (white part discarded)	⅓	cup flour
		½	cup red wine
		2	cups beef broth or bouillon
¼	pound fresh mushrooms, sliced	12	small white onions
		1	clove garlic, minced
½	stick butter		Salt and pepper

Sauté the beef kidneys in the butter with the mushrooms. Sprinkle with the flour and add the wine and broth slowly, stirring until smooth and thickened. Add onions and garlic and cook for 30–40 minutes over low heat. Serves 4 to 6.

S E R V E   W I T H

> Kasha with sea shells (p. 192)
> Cucumber with yogurt (p. 119)

SAUTÉED KIDNEYS IN FRENCH LOAVES

A sublime dish that makes your spirits soar.

2 small French loaves, brown-and-serve kind, cut in halves, lengthwise
4 tablespoons unsalted butter
2 veal kidneys, cut in pieces, or 6–8 lamb kidneys

¼ pound sliced fresh mushrooms
2 small cans Madeira sauce or 1 can beef gravy plus 2 tablespoons red wine
1 tablespoon brandy

Spread the halves of bread with some of the butter and brown in the oven. Sauté the kidneys and the mushrooms in the rest of the butter for about 5 minutes. Add the Madeira sauce and the brandy. Put one toasted half loaf on each plate and pour the kidney and mushroom mixture over it. Serves 4.

SERVE WITH

Cherry tomatoes and water cress

Other dishes using beef:
Finnish Stew (p. 93)
Armenian Melon (p. 68)
Polenta (p. 135)
Spaghetti and Italian Meat Sauce (p. 189)
Fried Rice (p. 211)

Other dishes using tongue:
Risi Pisi (p. 91)
Cold Ham Mousse (p. 92)
Sliced Meat Aspic (p. 94)
Fried Rice (p. 211)

VEAL MILANESE

There is nothing better than delicate and meltingly tender slices of veal that have been cooked briefly from 5 to 10 minutes. There is no need for convenience foods when you have veal and pasta fixed this way.

1½ pounds veal, cut for scal-   2 tablespoons butter
loppini and pounded thin   2 tablespoons olive oil
flour   ½ cup Marsala
Salt and pepper

You will have to ask around a bit until you find a butcher that knows how to cut paper-thin slices from the leg of veal. In a supermarket, ring the bell and ask. Ask him to pound it thin until it almost frays, or do it yourself, one piece at a time, between sheets of wax paper, with a potato masher or some other blunt instrument. Flour lightly on one side and salt and pepper on both. Put the floured side down in the skillet with a mixture of butter and olive oil, brown on one side and turn over on the other. This takes an incredibly brief amount of time. Pour a little Marsala in the pan the veal was cooked in and let it bubble up once or twice with the juices in the pan. Pour over the scalloppini on a hot platter and serve immediately. This is not a dish that is done ahead of time. Serves 4.

Green Pasta with Ricotta

1 package green or spinach   ¼ cup freshly grated Parmesan
noodles   or Romano cheese
½ cup whipped sweet butter   Salt and pepper
1 cup Italian ricotta, or less
delicately, cottage cheese

Have a deep pot of water boiling and pour in the noodles, which should be cooked at the last minute. Put in boiling, salted water and cook until barely tender. Meanwhile warm the ricotta and sweet butter and Parmesan in a pan, drain the noodles, and put on a warm platter. Pour the cheese and butter mixture over the noodles, tossing with a fork and spoon a bit to make sure it covers all of the pasta.

Large fresh mushroom caps,
stems chopped
Finely chopped parsley

Colonna's seasoned bread
crumbs

Brush the mushroom caps with melted butter inside and out, and heap the caps loosely with the mixture of the mushroom stems, parsley, and bread crumbs. Dot with butter and broil briefly just before serving.

SERVE WITH

> Green pasta with ricotta
> Stuffed mushrooms
> Water cress and lettuce salad with French dressing
> Italian bread

VEAL CUTLET OR CHOPS WITH PEAS

Veal, often overlooked as a choice, is always delicious and practically cooks itself. Here is an easy veal dish that needs no watching.

1½ pounds thick veal steak or
chops
3 tablespoons olive oil

1 package frozen peas
Pepper
Salt

Put the veal in a very heavy skillet with the olive oil on the bottom to keep from sticking. Add the frozen peas right from the package, and sprinkle with freshly ground black pepper. Cover tightly and bake in an oven preheated to 325° for 1 hour. That's all. Somehow the peas and the veal both end up tasting wonderfully of each other. Just before serving, sprinkle with salt. Serves 4.

SERVE WITH

> Pasta with anchovy sauce
> Salt sticks
> Fresh melon

VEAL SHOULDER

Once upon a time, long long ago, in the excitement of having my first garden of herbs, my husband and I sprinkled a veal roast with a finely chopped mixture of herbs before rolling and roasting. It was a beautiful roast with the delicate line of green, clean-tasting and delectable and—the strongest cathartic each of us had known. Now I'm older and wiser. Veal does indeed need knowing seasoning, but great restraint must be used.

Shoulder of veal, 3–4 pounds	10 small peeled white onions
3 tablespoons olive oil	1 bay leaf
1–1½ cups dry white wine	½ pound fresh mushrooms, sliced, or ¼ cup dried mushrooms, soaked
⅓ cup finely chopped parsley	2 egg yolks
½ teaspoon oregano	½ cup cream

Brown the shoulder of veal in the olive oil over high heat 5–10 minutes in a Dutch oven on the top of the stove. Then add the white wine, parsley, and oregano. Cover and reduce heat, and simmer about 1½ hours or until tender, basting from time to time and adding more wine if needed. The onions should be added after about one hour of cooking, and the bay leaf removed. The last half hour, add the mushrooms. Before serving, transfer the shoulder of veal and onions and mushrooms to a warm platter. Thicken the juices with the egg yolk mixed with cream, and serve separately or pour over the roast. Serves 4 to 6.

SERVE WITH

> Fresh peas
> Noodles Romanoff (bought packaged)
> Curly endive or chicory salad
> French bread

BAKED VEAL CHOPS IN MUSHROOM SAUCE

Americans who neglect veal—and lamb—are missing many delectable dishes. Europeans have long known how to add the proper seasoning and moist cooking that brings out the best in veal.

3 tablespoons bacon drippings or other fat
4 thick veal rib chops
3 tablespoons flour
1 can beef gravy
⅓ cup sherry wine
1 tablespoon Italian tomato paste

1 4-ounce can sliced broiled-in-butter mushrooms or ¼ pound fresh mushrooms, sliced and sautéed
Dash each thyme and marjoram
Minced garlic, salt and pepper to taste

Heat bacon drippings in a large, heavy skillet. Brown chops briefly on both sides. Remove chops from skillet. Add flour to drippings, stirring until well blended. Add beef gravy and wine; cook, stirring constantly, until mixture boils and thickens. Stir in tomato paste and then the mushrooms and seasonings. Add the chops, cover, and bake in a moderate oven (350° F.) for 1 hour or until meat is tender, turning and basting chops several times. Serves 4.

SERVE WITH

Tiny new potatoes, boiled and served in their skins
Ring mold of creamed spinach (frozen) with a center of diced peeled cucumbers, lightly mixed with mayonnaise or French dressing
Sesame sticks

SURI LEBERLI (SWISS LIVER)

Calves' liver, as cooked and served at the Swiss Pavilion in New York, is delicate and ambrosial, and quite a different dish entirely from our robust way with fried onions and bacon, good as that is. Calves' liver is best and the most expensive cooked this way, but baby beef liver is very good, too.

1½ pounds calves' liver or baby beef liver
2 tablespoons butter
1 tablespoon finely chopped onion

1 jigger white wine, preferably chablis
Salt and pepper
1 teaspoon freshly chopped parsley

Pour boiling water over the meat, and let stand 1 minute. Drain and cut liver into thin strips about 2 inches long. Sauté the meat in half of the butter over high heat for about 2 minutes. Add the onion and sauté another minute. Pour the wine over the meat. Light it with a match and let flame briefly. Add the remaining butter, sprinkle with salt, pepper and parsley. Serve immediately. Serves 4.

S E R V E W I T H

Green pasta with ricotta (p. 52)
Peas in butter sauce
Leaf lettuce salad with marinated cooked carrots and French dressing
Sesame seed rolls

BRATWURST WITH ZWIEBELKUCHEN

Bratwurst, a delicate veal sausage, is not easy to come by. It most likely will not be in pliofilm in your supermarket. Usually it is found only at German butchers who make a specialty of what we call cold-cuts, but it is worth a serious search. Traditionally, it is served and cooked with sauerkraut but this is a matter of individual taste. Simmer the bratwurst in water to cover for 20 minutes, and drain. Serve hot with German mustard.

Zwiebelkuchen

CRUST:

1 cup butter
2 cups flour

4 tablespoons milk
Salt and sugar

FILLING:

6 strips bacon, diced
4 large onions, diced
2 eggs plus 1 egg yolk
¾ cup sour cream

1 teaspoon chives, chopped
Salt and pepper
Pinch of caraway seed

To make the crust, mix ingredients gently together and put in refrigerator until dough is ready to be handled. Roll dough out and put in two 8" pie tins. Bake in a 350° oven for 10 minutes or until lightly browned.

Sauté the bacon until crisp, remove from pan. Pour off most of the fat, leaving a film on bottom of skillet, in which sauté the onions until opaque but not browned. Drain. Add the beaten eggs, drained and partially cooked onions, bacon, sour cream, seasoning, and chives, mixed together. Pour into pie crust, add caraway seeds, and bake in oven 350–375° for 15–20 minutes, or until a knife inserted comes out clean. Serve warm but not hot. Serves 4 generously.

SERVE WITH

Fresh fruit salad (p. 49)

CALVES' HEARTS STUFFED WITH
APRICOT AND ONION

Calves' hearts are to me one of the most delicious of all meats. I like them sliced and cooked briefly, but most of all I like them stuffed and roasted slowly. It does take time and sometimes, in some places, it takes time to find a store that sells them. Almost any butcher will get them for you if he knows you like them, and of course nowadays you can get lots and put them in the freezer.

2 calves' hearts (tubes, fat membrane, and fat cut out)	3 tablespoons butter
½ cup chopped dried apricots	1 cup dry white wine
1 medium-sized onion, chopped fine	or
1 teaspoon rosemary	1 cup bouillon plus juice of half lemon
	Salt and pepper

Stuff the hearts with a mixture of the apricots, onion, and rosemary. Sauté briefly in half of the butter and transfer to a small casserole that fits rather snugly. Dot the tops of the hearts with the rest of the butter and pour the wine into the casserole. Roast in a 350° oven for about an hour and a half or until the hearts are tender, basting occasionally with the juices in the casserole. Serves 4.

SERVE WITH

Baked sweet potatoes—break open and mash with butter, grated orange peel, and black walnuts
Pumpernickel bread

VEAL STEW

Veal is protean protein, sometimes bland and delicate, sometimes rich and savory. Among other things, it makes a delectable and texturally interesting stew.

2 pounds veal, cut up for stew
2 lemon wedges
Flour and pepper
4 tablespoons butter
¼ pound small button mushrooms
8 small onions

1 pound can tiny new potatoes, drained
1 cup dry white wine (½ cup at a time)
⅓ cup chopped fresh parsley
1 teaspoon celery flakes
Salt

Lightly flour and pepper the veal but do not add the salt until the end. Brown in butter and squeeze in the lemon juice. Brown the mushrooms and small onions in butter, separately. Add half a cup wine first, cover, and simmer. Brown the potatoes in the same pan, add to the veal, and add the rest of the wine, parsley, and celery flakes. Just before serving, add the salt and check the seasoning. Add more if desired. Serves 4.

French Fried Zucchini

Cut zucchini in fingers lengthwise, but do not peel. Dip in seasoned flour and fry in 1½ inches of deep fat at 350°. Fry a few at a time.

SERVE WITH

French fried zucchini
Hot butterflake rolls

GRILLED CALVES' TONGUES

Admittedly, small tender calves' tongues are not available in every market, so when you find them get a few extra to put in your freezer, after cooking them first. They are apt to run from slightly under a pound to slightly over.

2 calves' tongues
1 tablespoon mixed pickling spice
2 tablespoons prepared mustard, preferably French or German

4 tablespoons butter
4 tablespoons coarse toasted bread crumbs

Simmer the calves' tongues in water with the mixed pickling spice until tender, or until the little bones at the back wiggle loose. Let cool in the liquid, remove, and skin. Slice lengthwise in halves if the tongues are very small, in three lengthwise slices if they are slightly larger. Arrange the slices of tongue in a shallow casserole or baking dish. Spread top side with mustard. Melt the butter and dribble over the slices generously. Sprinkle lavishly with the bread crumbs, covering as completely as possible. If the tongues are long you may need more bread crumbs. Put under the broiler, about 3–4 inches from the flame until hot and sizzling. Serves 4 or more, depending on size of tongues.

SERVE WITH

Kugele with sour cream, (p. 194)
Beet and horse-radish salad
Hot butterflake rolls
Dried apricots soaked overnight in white wine and served with sour cream and slivered almonds

VEAL POT ROAST IN WHITE

Cooked this way, the veal has an unusual flavor and interesting texture.

3 pounds veal rump
3 tablespoons oil
2 medium-sized onions, quartered
1 bunch parsley, chopped

1 green pepper, cut in strips and seeds removed
2 cups or more dry white wine
Salt and pepper
1 package frozen lima beans

Brown the roast in the fat. Add the onions, parsley, salt, pepper, and wine. Cover and simmer about 2 hours with meat on a rack. About 30 minutes before done, add the lima beans, green pepper and more wine if necessary. Serves 4 to 6.

SERVE WITH

Green salad with vinaigrette dressing
Hot poppy seed rolls

Other dishes using veal:
Finnish Stew (p. 93)
Pastel de Choclo (p. 32)

Lamb

BARBECUED LAMB SHANKS

Plump, meaty lamb shanks are an interesting cut of meat to cook and to eat and yet not too many people are familiar with them. They need long, moist cooking and knowledgeable seasoning.

4 meaty lamb shanks	½ cup soy sauce
2 tablespoons olive oil	½ cup honey
½ cup brandy or half brandy, half sherry	1½ teaspoons salt

Heat the brandy, soy sauce, and honey together briefly just enough to blend. Marinate the lamb shanks in this mixture for 3–4 hours. Remove the shanks from the marinade, brown in the oil in a skillet on the stove. Transfer to a baking dish and add the marinade. Cover and cook in a 350° oven for 1½ hours, basting from time to time with the marinade. Serves 4.

SERVE WITH

> Baked potatoes
> Creamed spinach
> Chopped cucumbers in yogurt with chopped mint
> Hot sesame seed rolls

This is a South African version of an Indian dish. The skewered meat, served with curry accompaniments, is laid in a marinade. The skewers used are the small bamboo ones than can be bought in any Oriental store for a pittance a pack. The original recipe calls for mutton but we are a bit evasive about the ages of our lambs and sheep. Theoretically, we do not have any very old ones nor do we have many suckling lambs.

2 pounds lamb	1 green canned chile, chopped fine
2 tablespoons oil	
2 cloves garlic, minced	Cayenne pepper
2 large onions, sliced	1 teaspoon grated orange peel
6–8 whole canned, seeded apricots, puréed with ½ cup of the juice	2 tablespoons curry powder
	2 tablespoons brown sugar
	½ teaspoon salt
1 teaspoon dried hot Italian pepper, crumbled, or	3 tablespoons wine vinegar or lemon juice

Remove any fat from lamb and cut fat in half-inch squares. Cut the lamb in 1½-inch squares. String on the bamboo skewers and alternate the meat and the fat. Cook the onions and garlic in the oil until transparent and soft. Add the apricot purée, orange peel, curry powder, sugar, a pinch of cayenne pepper, salt, and vinegar. Stir well and bring to a boil for a minute or two. Lay the skewered meat in a shallow enamel or ceramic dish (not a metal one). Cool the sauce and pour over the meat. Let it marinate overnight or longer, turning the sassaties occasionally. Drain and broil over or under a hot fire, turning until brown on all sides. Heat the sauce and pour over the grilled sassaties. The Armenians push the meat off their skewers onto a warm platter before serving. Apparently the South Africans, with smaller skewers, do not. Serves 4.

SERVE WITH

Rice and curry accompaniments (p. 166)

BROILED MARINATED LAMB STEAKS

As anyone knows who has ever eaten in a Greek or Armenian restaurant, there is a special affinity between lamb and eggplant.

Marinate lamb steaks, cut from a leg of lamb by the butcher, in a shallow pan. Mix a marinade of 1 teaspoon of dry mustard, 1 teaspoon of salt, ½ teaspoon of freshly ground black pepper, ½ cup sherry, and ½ clove of garlic minced or one large onion. Rub the marinade into the steaks on both sides and pour the rest over the steaks. Cover and chill in the refrigerator for several hours. Remove from the refrigerator about ¾ hour before broiling and allow to come to room temperature. Set oven control to "very hot" (500–550°) and preheat broiler for 10 minutes. Rub broiler rack with lamb fat cut from the steaks. Arrange steaks on broiler rack 3 inches from the heat. Broil 5–6 minutes on each side for chops ¾ inch, 7–8 minutes for ones ⅞ inch. Baste with marinade left in pan. These may also be pan-broiled by heating the skillet very hot, and rubbing the pan with lamb fat cut from steaks. Sear the steaks on each side, lower heat, add some of the marinade, and cook 3–4 minutes longer on each side. Serve on hot platter with the drippings and the rest of the marinade over the chops. Surround with broiled or pan-fried orange slices. Sprinkle them lightly with sherry and brown sugar. They will become a light brown in 1–2 minutes. Garnish with water cress and mint.

Baked Eggplant with Cheese

1 medium-sized eggplant, peeled, diced, and soaked in salted water
2 tablespoons butter
2 tablespoons flour
½ cup milk
1 tablespoon lemon juice
1 cup grated cheddar cheese
¼ cup tomato catsup or chili sauce

2 eggs
Salt and pepper
½ cup chopped green onions, tops and bottoms,
   or
½ cup sliced fresh or canned mushrooms (nice but not obligatory)

Boil the eggplant in salted water for about 10 minutes. Mash or put in an electric blender until smooth, with the milk, flour, butter, and lemon juice. Remove from blender, stir in the grated cheese, catsup, eggs, and the scallions or mushrooms, if used. They are nice additions but not essential. Turn into a shallow buttered casserole and bake in a 350° oven 20–25 minutes or until puffy or slightly browned on top. This does make 4 usual-size servings but it is wise to double the recipe because most people want more.

SERVE WITH

> Baked eggplant with cheese
> Water cress and endive salad with French dressing, plus a teaspoon of minced onion, and a dash of paprika
> Poppy seed rolls

ROAST LEG OF LAMB

An unusual recipe for roast lamb, with different and interesting flavor.

1 leg of lamb (5–6 pounds)	2 tablespoons anchovy paste
Salt	⅔ cup tarragon

Rub the lamb with salt and anchovy paste. Put in a roasting pan in a 350° oven. Pour the vinegar over the lamb. Baste with the vinegar and fat mixture from time to time. The lamb will take about 3 hours. A meat thermometer inserted in the leg should read 140° for rare, 175° for well done.

SERVE WITH

> Plain Risi Pisi (top of p. 91)
> Sliced cucumbers
> Hot rolls

LAMB AND GREEN BEAN STEW

Naturally, in this dish, any cut green beans may be used, but the Italian green beans now on the market have a particularly pleasant crispness.

1½ pounds stewing lamb, cubed
1 cup sliced onions
2 tablespoons butter
2 cups beef bouillon
1½ cups diced raw potatoes
1 package frozen Italian green beans
2 green peppers, chopped and seeds removed

1 small can water chestnuts, sliced
Salt and pepper
1 teaspoon Worcestershire sauce
2 tablespoons butter and flour (2 tablespoons of each, mixed together)

Brown the lamb and onions in the butter. Add the bouillon and simmer 1½ hours or until the meat is almost tender. Add the potatoes, green beans, green peppers, water chestnuts, salt, pepper and Worcestershire sauce. Cook about 25 minutes more or until vegetables are done. Add the butter and flour mixture and cook 5 minutes longer, stirring constantly. Part of the preparation of this dish may be done ahead of time. It is best to cook the meat ahead, refrigerate and reheat with the vegetables at mealtime. Serves 4 to 6.

SERVE WITH

Sliced tomatoes sprinkled with finely chopped chives and parsley and marinated with French dressing
Hot biscuits

ROAST LEG OF LAMB, EUROPEAN STYLE

No one who has ever smelled a succulent leg of lamb roasting could be a vegetarian. It is an enticing aroma, as provoking as freshly baked bread or just roasted coffee.

5–6 pound leg of lamb, trimmed of excess fat	1½ tablespoons rosemary
2–4 cloves garlic	2 tablespoons butter
Freshly ground black pepper	½ cup olive oil
	½ cup Marsala wine

Cut the garlic in slivers and insert here and there in the leg of lamb, pushing in holes made with a skewer as far as possible. Rub the lamb with freshly ground black pepper and the rosemary. Melt the butter and mix with the olive oil and Marsala to use as a basting liquid. Brown the lamb in the oven at 400° for 10 minutes, then reduce temperature to 325° and cook for 2 hours for the European style (which means the lamb will be slightly pink) or until the meat thermometer registers 140°. Baste from time to time with the basting liquid. For the American way of cooking lamb, continue to roast until the thermometer registers 175° or until there is no pink. Serves 4 to 6.

SERVE WITH

Macaroni, cooked the usual way, and then, possibly baked in an Edam cheese shell as the Dutch do, deliciously and frugally, when they get towards the end of one—or otherwise, in a casserole with a cheese sauce.

Cooked artichoke hearts, frozen or canned, that have been rolled in Colonna's seasoned bread crumbs, sprinkled with oil and baked briefly.

Mixed green salad

All around the Mediterranean they put mixtures of meat and rice, or rice with pine nuts and currants, in green peppers, tomatoes, zucchini, and eggplant halves. The same mixture takes on a different flavor according to its vegetable container. One of the more unusual containers that gives a very fresh and different flavor to the mixture is a melon. It may be a honeydew, a Persian melon, or one very large cantaloupe or two small ones. The Armenians prefer the rice slightly crunchy. If a softer rice is preferred, precook for 10 minutes in boiling water and drain.

	Melon	½	cup uncooked rice
2	tablespoons butter	⅓	cup currants
½	pound ground lamb or beef	⅓	cup pignolias or pine nuts
1	medium-sized onion, chopped	⅓	cup white wine or water

Cut the lid off the top of the melon and scoop out the seeds and some of the flesh, leaving some in the melon. Sauté the meat and onion briefly in the butter, then mix with the other ingredients. Fill melon with this mixture, mixing with pieces of melon removed from the inside, and add the white wine. Put in a 350° oven and bake 50 minutes to an hour. The melon and wine, which is most unauthentic, should provide enough liquid. If it starts to dry out, add more wine or water. Serves 4. To serve, quarter by cutting from top to bottom. Serve warm.

SERVE WITH

French bread

CASSOULET OF LAMB WITH BLACK-EYED PEAS
AND ITALIAN GREEN BEANS

The only thing traditional about this cassoulet is that it has beans, lamb, and sausage. There the resemblance ends. It is, however, a happy blend of foods whether made with lamb from a cooked leg of lamb or starting from scratch with some lamb shoulder or lamb shanks.

2 cans cooked or 2 packages frozen black-eyed peas	2 medium-sized onions, chopped Fat if needed
2–3 cups cooked lamb, cut in thick chunks	2 packages frozen Italian green beans
½ pound sausage, preferably the Polish kalbassa	2 cans beef bouillon or bouillon cubes diluted in water
2 cloves garlic, minced	Worcestershire sauce

Sauté the pieces of lamb in a little fat. This is not strictly necessary but gives a little special flavor. Put in a deep casserole with the black-eyed peas that have been drained. Brown the sausage, onions, and garlic. Add to the casserole the bouillon and Worcestershire sauce. Cover and bake at 350° for one hour or more. The green beans are better with the briefer cooking so add 20 minutes before serving. This amount will serve 8 to 10 and tastes better the second day.

SERVE WITH

Grapefruit and lettuce salad
Salt sticks

LAMB WITH ORANGE AND BARLEY

Barley has recently been rediscovered, along with rice and wheat pilaf, as a welcome change from potatoes. It is a natural convenience food, needing no peeling or shelling or other preparation, takes very little space on the shelves, and is guaranteed not to sprout.

2 medium-sized onions, chopped
2 tablespoons butter or oil
1 pound lamb shoulder, cut in 2-inch squares,
   or
2 cups diced cooked lamb
1 cup pearl barley

3 oranges, sliced thin and seeds removed but not peeled,
   or
1 jar or can mandarin oranges, drained and the juice discarded
1 tablespoon lemon juice
3 cups beef bouillon

Sauté the onions and lamb shoulder in the fat, put in a medium-sized casserole with the barley, oranges, and half the liquid. Cover and bake at 300° and add the other half of the liquid. Cover tightly. Bake 45 minutes, add the rest of the bouillon, cover again, and bake 45 minutes longer or until done. Let stand 5–10 minutes before serving. Serves 4.

SERVE WITH

Belgian endive with a curry dressing—¼ cup olive oil, 1 tablespoon vinegar, 1 teaspoon curry powder, salt, and pepper
Sesame seed rolls

LAHMAJOON

This dish is in effect an Armenian hamburger baked simultaneously with its bun. In the traditional form, discs of raised dough made with olive oil as the shortening are baked with a mixture of chopped lamb and seasonings. The Armenian touch lies partly in the unusual seasoning—to us—of chopped fresh mint. This is a somewhat lazy way of doing the dish inasmuch as English muffins are substituted for the Armenian dough.

1 pound lamb shoulder, ground	½ cup Italian tomato paste
2 cups onion, chopped fine	½ can (1 pound) Italian plum tomatoes
¼ cup parsley, chopped	4 English muffins, split and toasted on split side
½ small green pepper, chopped	
1 teaspoon fresh mint leaves, chopped	

Mix all the ingredients together in a bowl with your fingers, kneading it thoroughly until the seasonings and the ingredients are well distributed with the lamb. Divide the mixture into eight parts and pat one part over each half of an English muffin. Spread mixture on the halves and place in an oven preheated to 400° and bake until the meat is cooked, about 10–15 minutes. Serves 4 (2 per person).

SERVE WITH

Bibb lettuce with lemon cream dressing (p. 107)

JELLIED MEAT LOAF

This meat loaf differs from most others, not only in the gelatin but because the basic meat is lamb with lamb tongues or veal. The lamb may be freshly cooked or made from leftovers from a roast leg of lamb. The tongue should be cooked from scratch because the stock is needed for the gelatin base.

2 pounds lamb shoulder and neck with bones, cut in chunks (or leftover leg of lamb)
2 lamb tongues or 1 veal tongue
1 medium-sized onion, peeled and quartered

1 stalk celery, chopped
Bay leaf
1 clove garlic, chopped
Salt and pepper
⅓ cup chopped fresh parsley
2 envelopes plain gelatin

Cook lamb shoulder, tongue, onion, celery, bay leaf and garlic in water until tender. This will vary according to the meat (at least 1 hour). Remove from liquid and separate meat from bones; skin tongue and dice both meats. Season with salt and pepper. Strain the liquid and measure. There should be three cups liquid; if necessary, add a mixture of water and white wine to complete the three cups. Put a layer of meat in a mold, sprinkled with chopped parsley. Repeat until all the meat is used. The top layer should be meat. Soften the gelatin in a half cup broth which has been cooled, add to the balance of the liquid, heat and stir until dissolved. Pour over the meat in the mold, tipping to make sure that it seeps through all parts, and chill until firm. Unmold and slice. This will serve 6 to 8.

SERVE WITH

    Curried vegetables (p. 201)
    Sliced cucumbers with vinegar dressing
    Pideh (Armenian flat bread)

LAMB WITH GRAPE GRAVY

This gravy has an unusual, sable hue that makes it look a little different from the usual brown gravy. It is a variant of the Cumberland sauce served with wild game. Any diced lamb, either cooked or uncooked, tastes better when heated in this gravy.

2 tablespoons fat	1 teaspoon dry English mustard
2–3 cups diced cooked lamb	1 teaspoon grated orange peel
or	1 can beef gravy
1–1½ pounds diced uncooked lamb	1 tablespoon Bourbon or brandy
½ cup grape jelly or spiced grape jam	

Sauté the lamb, cooked or uncooked, in the fat. Add the grape jelly and the mustard which has been mixed with 1 teaspoon water before adding. Add the orange peel, beef gravy, and Bourbon and stir until smooth. Cook over low heat for 20–30 minutes. Serves 4.

S E R V E   W I T H

> Mashed potatoes
> Grapefruit and orange salad
> Hot party rolls

Other dishes using lamb:
> Finnish Stew (p. 93)
> Risi Pisi (p. 91)
> Pastel de Choclo (p. 32)
> Biksemad (p. 39)

Pork and Ham

PORK CHOPS, CHINESE ROASTED

This uses as its basting liquid the same that is used with the Chinese roasted turkey on p. 140. The same mixture may be re-used if it has been refrigerated and is used within two weeks. Otherwise, start over again with this mixture in these smaller amounts.

½ cup soy sauce
¼ cup sherry
1 teaspoon sugar
1 slice fresh ginger or 1–2 pieces crystallized ginger and omit sugar

1 chopped scallion
8 thick pork chops

Boil first five ingredients together with 1 cup water. Let the pork chops rest in the marinade in the refrigerator for several hours. Remove from the refrigerator ½ hour before starting to cook. Bake 1 hour in the marinade at 300°. Remove from the marinade.

SERVE WITH

Sauerkraut, rinsed and heated with 1 cup sour cream stirred in before serving
Pumpernickel bread

CASSEROLE OF BLACK BEANS

Black beans, usually met with only as soup, are delectable in their plump, pretty, and individual ways. Unless you can find canned ones, they must be started from scratch, soaking and simmering until tender. This is time-consuming but not in the least laborious. This is a melting pot version to which several European dishes and one Brazilian one have lent some of their characteristics.

1 pound dried black beans
1 head of garlic
½ cup bouillon
½ cup red wine
1 cup sour cream
    water cress
1 large or 2 medium onions,
    preferably the red sweet
    ones
3 tablespoons olive oil

2 tablespoons vinegar
1 dry hot red pepper
    (you can use the one from
    mixed pickling spices)
    Salt and pepper
3 medium-sized fresh oranges,
    peeled and sliced thin cross-
    wise, sprinkled with freshly
    chopped mint and chilled

Soak the black beans overnight or for several hours. Simmer until tender, with the head of garlic. Remove the garlic and drain. This part of the cooking may be done ahead of time. Heat with the bouillon and red wine in a casserole, adding salt and pepper if the bouillon does not have sufficient flavor. Marinate the onions in the oil, vinegar, red and black pepper, and salt. Serve the beans in the casserole with separate bowls of sour cream, water cress, marinated onion and sliced orange, to be passed around as accompaniments to the beans. Serves 4 to 6.

SERVE WITH

Tongue or roast loin of pork
Hard rolls

ROAST LOIN OF PORK
BAKED WITH VEGETABLES

This roast is cooked in hard cider or ¾ cup cider plus ¼ cup apple-jack or brandy, along with the vegetables, and is an oven meal that needs little attention.

Roast Loin of Pork Baked with Vegetables

1 pork loin (10 rib)
6 green apples, peeled halfway down and cored
6 medium-sized potatoes, peeled
6 large onions, peeled

Salt and pepper
1 cup hard cider or ¾ cup cider and ¼ cup applejack or brandy
2 tablespoons butter blended with 2 tablespoons flour

Roast the loin of pork that has been well rubbed with salt at 350° for 2 hours. Place the vegetables alternately around the roast and roast 1 hour longer. Remove from the oven and place vegetables on a heated platter; let the meat stand 20 minutes, then carve and place in the center of the platter. Meanwhile, pour off fat in roasting pan and place pan over high heat. Add one cup boiling cider and the butter and flour mixture, and blend with a wire whip or a spoon. Mix with the pan glaze and dripping. Taste and correct the seasoning in the gravy. Serve the gravy from a sauce boat or low fat pitcher. Serves 6 to 8.

The apricot and horse-radish sauce is good not only with the roast pork but also with sliced tongue, roast or broiled turkey or duck, and is, of course, better made with the freshly grated horse-radish. This is not easy to come by unless you live in a big city with a market that sells it freshly grated, or else have a few roots in your own garden.

Apricot and Horse-Radish Sauce

1 cup puréed apricots (¼ cup juice and apricots from 1-pound can) put in a blender or mashed

2–3 tablespoons freshly grated horse-radish or 1½–2 bottles horse-radish

Mix together and chill. Makes about 1½ cups sauce.

SERVE WITH

Apricot and horse-radish sauce
Broccoli flowerets which have been boiled first and heated with 1 can of condensed cream of celery soup, with a dash of nutmeg
Poppy seed rolls

CHINESE PORK AND CELERY

Pork as cooked the Chinese way in their traditional dishes is a delicate and different meat from that in our more robust ones. The meat will be cooked sufficiently in this brief time when cut like this.

¾ pound lean pork, cut in strips ¼ x 2 inches
1 tablespoon cornstarch mixed with 1 tablespoon water
1 tablespoon soy sauce

¼ pound mushrooms, sliced
1 cup chopped celery
4 tablespoons butter
Very little salt (soy sauce has some)

Heat butter in skillet. Add mushrooms and celery and cook for 3 minutes or more. Add the pork strips and cook for 10 minutes more. Add soy sauce and cook 5 minutes more. Serves 4.

SERVE WITH

Rice
Spiced peaches

BELGIAN PORK CHOPS

Pork chops rubbed with a mixture of chopped onion, garlic, and parsley, browning on both sides, and then cooked in hard cider are served in both Belgium and parts of France. The hard cider gives the pork chops the same acid contrast one gets with apples and sour cherries, only a little better. However, hard cider is not easy to come by these days and what is labeled cider and pasteurized is apt to be rather bland apple juice. To approximate more or less the hard cider, add a few tablespoons of applejack, brandy, or whiskey to the sweet cider.

4 pork chops, with the fat slashed	Salt, pepper, and olive oil
1 small onion	1 cup cider
½ clove garlic	2–3 tablespoons applejack, brandy, or whiskey
1 tablespoon finely chopped parsley	

Mix the onion, garlic, and parsley together and rub on each side of the pork chops. Sprinkle with salt and pepper; brush with olive oil. Either broil on each side or pan-broil on top of stove. Pour on the cider, bring to a boil, cover, and turn down heat until chops are tender and the juices of the meat have formed a sauce with the cider. Remove top, stir in applejack or equivalent, simmer a few minutes, and serve. Serves 4.

SERVE WITH

>Brussels sprouts, cooked in chicken broth with butter and white grapes added
>Sweet potatoes baked in their jackets
>Corn sticks

PORK CHOPS "STUFFED" WITH PENNSYLVANIA DUTCH POTATO "FILLING"

This filling is more apt to be on top of the pork chops than inserted in the chops.

¾ cup bread crumbs, dried but not toasted in the oven
3 tablespoons butter
⅓ cup finely chopped celery
⅓ cup finely chopped onion

1½ cups mashed potatoes
1 egg
Salt and pepper
4 thick loin pork chops

Sauté the bread crumbs, celery, and onion in the butter. Add the parsley and mix with the mashed potatoes, egg, and seasonings. Sauté the chops on one side and then turn over so that the cooked side is up. Pile the cooked side with the potato mixture. Arrange in a shallow casserole and bake in a 350° oven for about an hour, basting from time to time with the pork juice. The potato mixture should be lightly browned. Serves 4.

SERVE WITH

Small zucchini—cut in half and hollowed out, filled with small pieces of butter and Parmesan cheese, skewered together, and baked in a casserole with tomato sauce until tender.
Marinated chick peas or garbanzos or ceci—drain and chill in French dressing with finely chopped onion and parsley
Armenian bread

SCALLOPED POTATOES WITH PORK CHOPS

This is filling and heartening on a cold, shivery day and involves little wear and tear on the cook, who is probably cold, too. The chops may be browned ahead of time and kept in the refrigerator until ready to add to the casserole.

2 cups thinly sliced raw potatoes	4 loin or rib pork chops (½–¾ inch thick)
6–8 spiced crab apples, diced	4 tablespoons flour
1 small onion, sliced	1 cup milk
1 teaspoon salt	Pepper

Arrange potatoes (either packaged dehydrated or cold boiled sliced), crab apples, and onion in layers in a greased baking dish, seasoning each layer with salt and pepper. Trim fat from chops and save for later use. Lightly season each chop with salt and pepper and coat well with 3 tablespoons of the flour. Brown chops on both sides in some of the fat in a frying pan. When chops are well browned, remove them from the pan. Set aside all except 1 tablespoon of fat from frying pan. Mix the remaining 1 tablespoon flour with the fat in the pan. (Avoid scraping off any browned flour from pan which may give a burned taste.) Add milk and blend. Cook, stirring well until the sauce is smooth, but still thin. Pour sauce over potatoes in baking dish. Top with browned chops, cover, and bake at 350° for 50–60 minutes. Serves 4.

SERVE WITH

Green peas and mushrooms (frozen)
Crusty hard rolls

PORK TENDERLOIN

The tenderloin is the center piece cut from a line of pork chops. It's the same meat, but boneless, fatless, and delicious.

1½ pounds tenderloin	2 tablespoons cornstarch
1 clove garlic, minced	1 can sour pie-cherries
1 medium-sized onion, diced	2 tablespoons sugar
2 tablespoons butter	
½ green pepper, cut in inch squares	

Put the tenderloin in a casserole, roast at 450° for ten minutes, then reduce heat to 350° and roast 35 minutes more. Meanwhile, sauté the garlic and onions in the butter and add the green pepper. Mix the cornstarch with some of the juice from the cherries, stir until smooth, and add the sugar and cherries. Add thickened and sweetened cherries to the garlic and green pepper mixture. Pour over the pork tenderloin and roast 15 minutes more or until a meat thermometer inserted in the meat reaches an internal temperature of 185°. The over-all time should be from 1 to 1½ hours. Serves 4.

S E R V E   W I T H

Cooked kasha or mashed potatoes
French fried onion rings
Water cress salad

GLAZED PORK LOIN

Pork loin, the aristocrat of the pork family, is especially good when glazed and served with unusual baked apples.

1 loin (4–5 pounds) of pork	Freshly ground black pepper
2 cloves garlic, finely chopped	Salt
1 tablespoon oregano	⅔ cup brown sugar
3 tablespoons olive oil	1 tablespoon cinnamon
2 tablespoons lemon juice	

Mix the garlic, oregano, olive oil, and lemon juice with salt and pepper to taste. Rub the mixture into the pork loin on all sides. Preheat oven to 350°, and put the pork loin on a rack in an uncovered roasting pan. Roast for 2½ hours or until a meat thermometer inserted in the meat registers 185°. After the meat has been roasting for about 2 hours, remove from the oven and roll in the mixture of brown sugar and cinnamon. Return to the oven for ½ hour until meat is done and there is a nice brown glaze. Serves 6 to 8.

SERVE WITH

> Baked sweet potatoes
> Baked apples (fill the centers with pine nuts, grated lemon peel, and brown sugar, dot with butter, and baste with white wine)
> Poppy seed rolls

BAKED HAM OR HAM SLICE WITH CORN PUDDING

This variation of corn pudding combines well with ham. The green chiles which are available in cans in most supermarkets should be added to dishes cautiously until you have found the amount pleasing to you and your family. They are very hot.

Corn Pudding (Southwestern Style)

2 cans niblet corn, drained
1 can condensed cheddar cheese soup
2 or 3 green chiles (canned), diced

1 medium-sized onion (chopped fine)
3 eggs, separated

Mix the niblet corn and the green chile, onion and cheddar soup, stir in the egg yolks, beat the whites until stiff and fold in. Put in a buttered small casserole and bake 40–45 minutes in a 350° oven. Serves 4 to 6.

Cole Slaw with Cream Dressing

½ small head cabbage, shredded
½ cup sour cream or heavy cream, whipped

1 tablespoon lemon juice
1 teaspoon or more sugar

Mix and toss together. The exact proportions for this slaw vary slightly according to the flavor and size of the cabbage. Some are sweeter than others.

SERVE WITH

Baked ham or ham slice
Corn pudding (Southwestern style)
Cole slaw with cream dressing
Hot biscuits

GLAZED CANADIAN BACON

Canadian bacon is pork loin that has been smoked in a special way and does not always come from Canada. While it is often sold sliced, it may also be bought in a piece and treated much as one does a pork loin. It makes a rather handsome dish. It is also good for small-sized families.

1 pound Canadian bacon or more

1 jar puréed apricots (for babies) or 8 canned apricots mashed with a bit of juice

1 teaspoon freshly grated lemon peel

2 tablespoons brandy or Bourbon

2 tablespoons brown sugar

Arrange the piece of Canadian bacon in a small casserole that fits fairly snugly. Mix the puréed apricots with the grated lemon peel and brandy or Bourbon and coat the piece of bacon thickly. Sprinkle generously and as evenly as possible with the brown sugar. Roast in a 400° oven about 30 minutes, adding a little wine or orange juice to the bottom of the casserole if it starts to cook dry. Serves 4.

SERVE WITH

Baked sweet potatoes
Water cress with thin slices of orange, peeled, thin slices of raw onion, and French dressing, and sprinkled with wrinkled, pitted black Greek olives
Rye rolls

HAM SLICE WITH BAKED ONION AND PEANUTS

This is a mostly all-in-the-oven meal. If your oven is small, perhaps you had better pan-broil the ham slice on the top of the stove. The onions and peanuts go very well together, whether the onions are fresh and sliced, or canned and whole. (The frozen chopped onions do not work well in this dish as they are too watery.)

Baked Onion and Peanuts

3½ cups sliced or diced onions   3 tablespoons flour
     or 2 cans (#1) small boiled   ¾ cup milk
     onions, drained   1 cup peanuts, chopped
 3 tablespoons butter

Cook the onions in a little water until barely tender, drain, and save half the liquid. Make a cream sauce as follows: Melt the butter and add the flour, stirring until smooth. Add the onion liquid and milk, stirring until smooth and thickened. Mix with the onions and put a layer in the bottom of a buttered baking dish. Sprinkle with peanuts and repeat the layers, topping with peanuts. Bake until browned on top, about 25 minutes. Serves 4.

SERVE WITH

Baked acorn squash
Asparagus salad
Poppy seed rolls

MARYLAND STUFFED HAM

Traditionally, this is served at Easter in St. Mary's County, Maryland, and the greens that are used as stuffing vary from cook to cook. The ham is supposed to be a year-old country ham. Older than that, it would be too hard to stuff, and the old cooks neither knew nor liked the ones you get in the supermarket. This is admittedly an adaptation, and is best made, in lieu of the scarce and hard-to-find country ham, with a Dutch, Danish, or Polish canned one.

1 ham, 3–5 pounds canned (Danish, Dutch, or Polish)
2 pounds fresh packaged spinach, chopped
3–4 green onions, finely chopped
½ cup chopped mint leaves
1 teaspoon red pepper
Salt

Mix the spinach, onions, mint leaves, red pepper, and salt together. Drop in boiling water and drain immediately. Open the ham and make a number of holes in it with knife or carving steel. Poke the mixture inside the holes with your fingers or whatever is convenient to use. The old way was to sew the country ham in cheesecloth and boil. The new way is to wrap in aluminum foil and bake for a couple of hours at 350°. Serve at room temperature. The servings depend upon the size of the ham. A three-pound one will serve 6 to 8.

SERVE WITH

Hominy
Fresh asparagus with Hollandaise sauce
Hot biscuits

EGG MOLD WITH CAVIAR DRESSING

This is a handsome dish to make in a ring mold and serve with the stuffed Maryland ham (p. 86). It is of European derivation, as indeed are most of our dishes, if not all our ingredients.

12–14 hard-cooked eggs
  1 green pepper, chopped fine, with seeds and white membrane removed
  1 small can chopped pimientos
  Salt and pepper

  1 teaspoon Worcestershire sauce
  1 tablespoon finely chopped onion
  Mayonnaise (*not* salad dressing)
  Leaf lettuce
  Thousand Island dressing
  Caviar, black or red, or capers

Chop the eggs fine, and mix with the green pepper, chopped pimientos, salt, pepper, Worcestershire sauce, onion, and enough mayonnaise to make a firm mixture. Pack into a 5-cup ring mold and refrigerate overnight. Unmold on torn leaf lettuce. Serves 4 to 6. Mix the dressing with the caviar or capers and serve with the egg mold.

SERVE WITH

Stuffed Maryland ham (p. 86)
Hot butterflake biscuits

This decorative way of serving sliced or diced, cooked, or canned ham, jellied on the serving platter, is a modified version of the French jambon persillé. The capellini served with this is a very fine pasta; it takes just 1–2 minutes to cook and should be dipped in and dipped out of the boiling salted water quickly, then drained, and dressed with olive oil that has been heated with a clove or two of garlic. Sprinkle over the dish about ¾ of a cup of coarsely chopped walnuts.

Sliced cooked or canned ham	Bourbon
1–2 packages apple-flavored gelatin	⅓ cup finely chopped fresh frozen parsley

Use a slightly curved (in depth) handsome platter—glass, if available. Arrange the slices of ham in a circle, overlapping symmetrically. Prepare the apple gelatin according to the directions on the box but substituting ¼ cup Bourbon for part of the liquid in each package. Add the parsley and chill until the thickness of egg whites. Pour over the ham in the platter which has also been chilling. Chill until firm. Remove from the refrigerator just before serving. One package of apple gelatin will be enough for a moderate number of slices of ham for 6 people.

S E R V E W I T H

Capellini with olive oil, garlic, and walnuts
Water cress salad with thin-sliced oranges and onions with French dressing (2 parts olive oil, 1 part vinegar, salt, pepper, and ½ teaspoon dry English mustard)

HAM WITH RED-EYE GRAVY

There is a very good reason why Southern country hams have so much better flavor and texture than the pre-cooked, water-injected and practically pre-digested hams found in the supermarket. For one thing, Southerners care more about ham, and take the trouble to search for the good ones. It takes time to find them, to cook them as they should be cooked, and, alas, money. There is a way that the Southerners cook slices of ham with what is sometimes called ham gravy and other times red-eye gravy. Even slices from the supermarket hams taste better with this treatment.

1 slice baking ham, preferably   2 tablespoons ham fat
   1¼ pounds   1 tablespoon strong coffee
   Sugar

Cut the skin from around the ham steak and grease a heated skillet with the fat. Sauté the ham over low heat until brown on each side, sprinkling each side with a little sugar before cooking. Remove to a warm platter. Pour 2 tablespoons of the ham fat into a gravy boat or fat pottery pitcher. Brown the rest in the skillet. Add the coffee, ½ teaspoon sugar, and the ½ cup of water, and bring to a boil. Pour into the fat in the gravy boat and serve. Serves 4.

SERVE WITH

> Frozen tiny new potatoes cooked in butter and finely chopped parsley
> Glazed onions—small white onions cooked, or drained canned, sautéed in butter until pale gold, sprinkled with sugar, covered with bouillon, and simmered until liquid is almost evaporated and onions are beginning to be caramelized
> Wilted lettuce salad
> Corn bread

HAM AND SPINACH AU GRATIN

This is a rather free adaptation of a French dish that works very well using frozen creamed spinach.

2 packages frozen creamed spinach
8 slices cooked ham (not too thin)
2 tablespoons butter
2 tablespoons flour
½ cup chicken broth

½ cup light cream
½ cup grated Switzerland Swiss cheese
¼ cup freshly grated Parmesan
1 jigger brandy or Bourbon
Salt and pepper

Let the frozen creamed spinach thaw slightly. Arrange a layer on the bottom of a medium-sized casserole, then 4 slices of ham, overlapping if necessary. Make a sauce by melting the butter, stirring in the flour, and cooking for a minute or two to get rid of the flour taste. Add the chicken broth, a little at a time, stirring until smooth, and then the cream. Stir in the cheese, brandy, salt, and pepper, and put half of the mixture on top of the ham. Add another layer of creamed spinach and ham and top with the rest of the sauce. Bake in a 350° oven about 20 minutes or until lightly browned. Serves 4.

SERVE WITH

Paraguayan corn bread (p. 32)
Grapefruit segments in lemon gelatine.

RISI PISI

Risi Pisi in its more or less classic version is rice cooked with onion and broth, and fresh peas and grated Parmesan added. Sometimes some beef marrow is added. In this one, meat has been added with the pimientos to make it a meal in itself.

⅓ cup onions, finely chopped
2 tablespoons butter
1½ cups long-grain rice
1 tablespoon warm dry white wine
3 cups hot beef consommé
1 cup fresh or frozen cooked peas

1½ cups diced cooked ham, tongue, or lamb
½ cup freshly grated Parmesan or Romano cheese
2 whole pimientos, diced, or 1 small jar of chopped
¼ cup finely chopped parsley
Salt and pepper

Cook the onions in the butter until lightly colored. Add the rice and stir around in the butter and onion mixture until opaque. Add the consommé and wine, bring to a boil, cover, and turn heat down very low. Cook 15–20 minutes, remove from the fire, fluff with a fork, and add the peas, ham, cheese, pimientos, and parsley. Add more salt and pepper if necessary, as some consommés are more highly seasoned than others. Serves 4.

SERVE WITH

Endive stalks with Roquefort dressing
Butterflake rolls

HAM AND SCALLOPED POTATOES

This uses the uncooked ham usually bought in steaks or slices.

1½ cups diced raw ham
1 package frozen Italian
   green beans
3 eggs

1 can chicken curry soup plus
   one can milk
4 medium-sized potatoes, peeled
   and sliced thin

In a medium-sized casserole, layer the potatoes, then the green beans and the ham, and repeat until all ingredients are used. Beat the eggs and mix with the chicken curry soup and the milk and pour over the casserole. Cover and cook for 1–1¼ hours, or until the potatoes are done. For the last 15 minutes, remove the lid. Serves 4.

SERVE WITH

Salad of individual mounds of grated raw carrot mixed with mayonnaise, approximately 4 or 5 mandarin oranges in segments arranged symmetrically leaning up against each mound.
Corn muffins

COLD HAM MOUSSE

If you wish a mousse of a velvety smooth texture, like the most elegant of pâtés, and you have an electric blender, put the ham and tongue in the blender; if not, pound or grind until smooth.

2 cups diced cooked lean
   mildly flavored ham
¼ pound cooked diced tongue
1 envelope unflavored gelatin

½ cup dry white or rosé wine
1 pint sour cream
1 teaspoon grated lemon peel

Put the ham and the tongue in the electric blender with the heated half cup of wine a cup of boiling water and lemon peel. Blend until smooth. If you do not have a blender and put it through a meat grinder or chop by hand very fine, soften the gelatin in 2 tablespoons cold water and dissolve in ½ cup boiling water. Mix with the ham and tongue mixture and wine and lemon peel; add the sour cream. Put in a 5-cup mold rinsed first with cold water, and chill until firm. Serves 4 to 6.

SERVE WITH

French bread
Spiced peaches or crabapples
Tiny new potatoes boiled and served in their skins with sour cream and chives

FINNISH STEW

In Finland one does not have to hunt for pieces of meat in the stew because it is all meat and all kinds, cooked together for a long time for lavish eating.

1 pound lean pork, cubed	2 or more teaspoons salt
½ pound lean beef, cubed	1 teaspoon coarsely ground
½ pound lean veal, cubed	black pepper
½ pound lean lamb, cubed	1 bay leaf
1 large onion, quartered	

Put in a casserole or Dutch oven with enough water to cover. Cook for 5–6 hours in an oven preheated to 325°. Serve in a casserole. Serves 4 to 6.

SERVE WITH

Baked potatoes
Sliced pickled beet salad
Dark pumpernickel bread and unsalted butter

SLICED TONGUE, HAM AND CHICKEN IN ASPIC

Professional chefs usually present cold sliced meats for a buffet on a platter with clear and shimmering and lovely coats of aspic. The dish is often decorated between coatings with a design, say of pimiento stars (using a tiny cutter), and the platter marked into quarters with thin slices of pitted ripe olives. It is simple for the home cook to do.

Sliced cooked chicken, tongue, turkey, or ham
2 tablespoons Maggi aspic jelly
1 cup boiling water

1 cup hot white wine
Pimientos, cut in stars or hearts, etc., with tiny cutters
Ripe olives, sliced and pitted

Arrange any boned sliced meat in an overlapping and symmetrical design on a platter and chill thoroughly. Dilute the Maggi aspic in the boiling water and white wine. Chill until the consistency of unbeaten egg whites. Pour a thin layer over the chilled meat and chill until firm. If desired, decorate with hearts or stars cut with tiny cutters from whole pimientos, and make a design, possibly by quartering the platter with thin slices of pitted ripe olives. Repeat with a second layer, softening the remaining jelly by heating if it becomes too hard. How many this will serve depends upon how much meat you have on the platters. This is enough aspic to decorate a moderate-sized platter that will serve 6 to 8.

SERVE WITH

Spinach soufflé (p. 113) or avocado mousse (page 207)
Hot biscuits

A RING MOLD OF HAM

When there is a cooked ham and a cooked turkey in the refrigerator or freezer, one is amply prepared for whatever fate may bring. There are so many ways to present ham that one need never wonder how to use it up.

3 cups ground ham	¼ cup catsup
⅔ cup dried quick oats	1 small onion, chopped
⅔ cup milk	Salt, pepper, and oregano
1 egg	

Soak the oats in the milk. Mix all the ingredients together, adding a little salt and pepper and oregano judicially, remembering that the ham is usually already salty. Pat lightly into a greased five-cup ring mold and bake in a medium oven about an hour. Serves 4.

SERVE WITH

Creamed potatoes in center of mold (p. 194 or use packaged dehydrated creamed potatoes)

Red cabbage slaw with diced spiced crab apples, sour cream dressing (1 cup sour cream plus 2 tablespoons lemon juice and 1 tablespoon prepared mustard)

Rye bread rolls

CASSEROLE OF GARBANZOS AND SAUSAGE

Garbanzos, or chick peas, or ceci, should be better known than they are, a lusty, sustaining legume amenable to many ways of cooking and seasoning. They can be bought canned very inexpensively, thus eliminating long soaking and seasoning. This is one of many ways of using them. They may be baked in any good rich spaghetti sauce.

2 cloves garlic, chopped
2 medium-sized onions, chopped
⅓ cup olive oil
2 green peppers, chopped, seeds and white membrane removed

⅓ cup parsley, chopped
3 cans tomato sauce
1 pound Italian sweet sausage
2 cans garbanzas or ceci, drained

Sauté the onion and garlic in the olive oil, add the green peppers, parsley, and tomato sauce. Remove the sausage from its skin and add to the tomato sauce. Put in a casserole with the garbanzos and bake 1–1¼ hours, at 350°. Serves 4 to 6.

SERVE WITH

Avocado and grapefruit segment salad with French dressing
French bread

POTATO AND SAUSAGE PIE

The original Pennsylvania Dutch version had a top and bottom crust of pie dough. This version is more suited to the streamlined figure, although even this would never be found on a reducing diet.

1 7-ounce package instant mashed potatoes (prepared according to directions but using all milk instead of part water)
2 tablespoons butter
2 eggs

3 tablespoons finely chopped parsley
1 large green pepper, seeds removed and coarsely chopped
1 pound lean pork sausage (preferably Gwaltneys from Smithfield, Va.)

Lightly and slightly sauté the sausage. Add parsley and green pepper. Mix the mashed potatoes with the unbeaten eggs and the butter. Put half the mixture in the bottom of a shallow casserole. Spread with the sausage mixture and top with the rest of the potatoes.

SERVE WITH

Chopped pickled beet salad with white grapes and French dressing
Poppy seed rolls

HAM AND GARBANZO SOUP

In Spanish it is garbanzo, in Italian it is ceci and in American it is chick peas. By whatever name it is called it is a legume, shaped like a hazelnut with an appealing, crunchy texture. This soup, which might even be called a stew, is a meal in itself and needs only a good French bread and a crisp fresh-tasting salad to complement it.

1 ham bone	peeled and diced
1 cup cubed cooked ham	2 bay leaves
1 large onion, chopped	1 pinch saffron
1 large can garbanzos (see above)	Salt and pepper
3 medium-sized potatoes, raw,	1 package frozen Italian green beans

Put the ham bone, ham, onion, garbanzos, potatoes, bay leaves, saffron, salt, and pepper in a soup pot or deep casserole with water to cover. Simmer for 1 hour, add the Italian green beans, and simmer 10–15 minutes more, or until the beans are done. Remove the ham bone and serve from deep casserole or tureen in deep soup plates. Serves 4 generously.

SERVE WITH

Cucumber, white grapes, water cress salad with French dressing
French bread

PORTUGUESE SOUP (ACCORDING TO CAPE COD)

This ham, potato and bean soup is a lusty, filling soup for a cold day or for those with hearty appetites on any day. The tablespoon of allspice is *not* a typographical error but an interesting flavor emphasis.

1 cup diced cooked, or raw ham
3–4 small onions, sliced
3 tablespoons bacon fat
6–7 medium-sized diced potatoes or 1 package frozen peeled new potatoes
1 family-sized can red kidney beans

1 clove garlic, minced
2 bay leaves
1 can Italian tomato paste
1 tablespoon whole allspice
2 cups consommé (bouillon cubes diluted in boiling water may be used)

Sauté the onions in bacon fat until pale yellow but not brown. Add the onions, kidney beans in their juice, garlic, bay leaves, potatoes, and ham. Dilute the tomato paste with consommé, and add to the soup. Add 3 or more cups of water as needed. Simmer together for at least 2 hours. Serves 4 to 6.

SERVE WITH

Tossed green salad
French bread

LIVER MOUSSE IN ASPIC

Liver mousse is a dish halfway in character between our rather rugged ways of serving and eating liverwurst, and fine European pâtés.

2 tablespoons gelatin
¼ cup white wine or Bourbon
2 cups canned jellied madrilene
1 pound liverwurst, softened at room temperature and skinned

½ stick butter, softened at room temperature
Nutmeg, salt, and pepper
1 cup sour cream

Soften the gelatin in the wine. Heat the soup and stir in the wine or Bourbon and gelatin, stirring until it is dissolved. Cool to lukewarm. Pour one cup of the soup into a chilled 1-quart mold and tip it around so that it coats all the sides. Chill for 10–15 minutes, and repeat until the coating on the mold is about ½ inch deep. Mash liverwurst with the butter and seasonings—a pinch of each—until smooth, add 1 cup of the soup and the sour cream, and pile into the coated cold mold. Put the mold in the refrigerator. Just before serving, unmold the liver onto a small cold platter, preferably glass to emphasize the lovely shimmering look. Serves 8.

SERVE WITH

Dandelion salad (p. 193)
Hot clover-leaf rolls

ITALIAN RED KIDNEY BEANS
WITH SPINACH AND PIGNOLIAS

This may be served as a reasonably hearty one-dish meal with the addition of some crumbled bacon or pieces of ham, or as a splendid and colorful side dish that needs only brief cooking.

⅓ cup olive oil
2 fat cloves garlic, minced
2 packages frozen chopped spinach
⅓ cup pignolias
Salt and pepper

1 family-sized can red kidney beans, drained
6 slices cooked crumbled bacon (used when the ham is not served)

Cook the garlic and spinach briefly in the oil. Add the pignolias and seasonings, and then the beans and the bacon, if used. Heat through and serve. Serves 4 to 6.

SERVE WITH

Broiled ham (optional)
Hot sesame seed rolls—from a refrigerated tube

Other dishes using pork:
Beef and Pork Goulash (p. 22)
Sarma (p. 30)
Siamese Curry (p. 26)
Chili con Carne (p. 29)
Empanadas (p. 44)
Biksemad (p. 39)
Spaghetti and Italian Meat Sauce (p. 189)
Fried Rice (p. 211)

Other dishes using ham:
Beef Tongue with Ham Sauce (p. 45)
Maryland Fried Chicken (p. 108)
Chicken Rolls (p. 120)

Chicken, Duck and Turkey

ROAST CHICKEN WITH LEMON

The delicate flavor of chicken is much enhanced by the acid emphasis of fresh lemon.

1 roasting chicken, about 4 pounds
1 tablespoon soy sauce
2 tablespoons sugar

¼ cup dry white wine
1 lemon, sliced very thin
¼ cup melted butter

Rub the inside and out of the chicken with the soy sauce. Mix the sugar, wine, and melted butter together, and brush over the chicken. Place the lemon slices on either side of the chicken in a pleasing design. Put on rack in small roasting pan and bake at 350°—30 minutes to the pound—basting from time to time with the liquid. The sugar helps to make a fine glaze, rather than sweetening. Serves 4 to 6.

SERVE WITH

Fresh peas
Belgian endive dipped leaf by leaf in olive oil and salt
Spoonbread (p. 191)

STEWED CHICKEN WITH CORN MEAL DUMPLINGS

We are catching and killing our chickens so young these days that a chicken stew with dumplings is becoming a half-remembered pleasure from one's childhood, depending, of course, on how long ago that was.

1 stewing chicken, 4–4½ pounds, cut in serving pieces (one used to say hen but, in these days of packaged chickens, one seldom knows the sex)
Salt

1 tablespoon crushed peppercorns
1 medium-sized onion, chopped
1 stalk celery, chopped
1 carrot, chopped
Corn meal dumplings
3 tablespoons flour

Wash the pieces of chicken under cold running water. Put in a Dutch oven or other heavy deep pan, and barely cover with water. Add the peppercorns and a little salt, and the chopped vegetables. Bring to a boil, then reduce the heat and simmer gently until the meat begins to fall from the bones, which with our pampered chickens should be no more than 2 hours. Fifteen minutes before serving, drop the corn meal dumplings into the simmering liquid. Cover tightly and cook 12–15 minutes without looking. Transfer the dumplings to a heated deep platter or casserole, and thicken the stew with the flour mixed with a little water. Serve immediately. Serves 4 to 6.

Corn Meal Dumplings

1 egg
¼ cup milk
½ cup sifted flour

½ teaspoon salt
1 teaspoon baking powder
½ cup corn meal

Beat the egg and add milk and beat together. Sift the flour, baking powder, and salt together and add the corn meal, which doesn't need sifting. Add the liquid to the dry ingredients, and drop by spoonfuls into the hot soup. Cover tightly and cook 12–15 minutes.

SERVE WITH

Cole slaw—shredded red cabbage and white grapes with Roquefort and sour cream dressing

CHICKEN IN BUTTER

In Denmark, where you can buy baby chickens that seem to us too young to be away from their mothers or even an impersonal brooder, they are roasted with a large lump of butter in the cavity and a handful of chopped parsley. It is a wonderfully simple dish and wonderfully good. The same method can be used for Rock Cornish hens or frying-size chickens.

1 chicken, about 2½ pounds, cut in quarters, or	½ pound (2 sticks) unsalted butter
4 Rock Cornish hens	2 egg yolks
	Salt and pepper

Skin the pieces of chicken and sauté briefly in half the butter, being careful that the chicken does not get brown. Transfer the chicken and the rest of the butter to a casserole with a tightly fitted lid. Bake 45 minutes at 325°. Transfer the pieces of chicken to a hot platter and remove the juices from the fire; add the beaten egg yolks. Return to low heat briefly until thickened, stirring with a whisk. Season with salt and pepper, and pour over chicken. Serves 4.

S E R V E   W I T H

Green pasta with cheese (p. 52)
Broiled mushroom caps
Broiled tomato halves

CAPTOLADE OF ROAST FOWL

I am not sure just what Captolade means, but it is a word used by Thomas Jefferson for this dish which he suggested serving for breakfast. It makes a good supper dish in our more effete times when heated or cooked and served over waffles, preferably made from scratch or a good ready-mix, although in an emergency the frozen ones may be used.

3 cups left-over roast fowl or a rotisserie chicken, diced
2 tablespoons butter
1 tablespoon chopped herbs, possibly basil, marjoram, and mint, or ½ teaspoon dried oregano

1 tablespoon flour
1 cup chicken gravy (canned)
1 wine glass white wine
Waffles, according to presumed capacities

Simmer all the ingredients together for 10–15 minutes. Serves 4.

SERVE WITH

Waffles
Raw celery stuffed with Roquefort cheese

PERSIAN CHICKEN

Presumably what makes this seem Persian is the orange peel flavoring and the almonds.

1 stick butter (¼ pound)
2 packages yellow rice (1 box)
1 barbecued chicken, meat removed from the bones and cut in serving size pieces
4 cups chicken broth

⅓ cup slivered almonds
½ teaspoon dried orange peel
 or
2 tablespoons chopped candied orange peel

Cook the rice in the butter over low heat until it is opaque. Add the chicken and chicken broth and the orange peel. Bring the rice and chicken mixture to a boil, cover, turn heat down, and simmer about 35 minutes. Remove lid, stir in almonds, and fluff with a fork. Serves 4.

SERVE WITH

Lettuce with lemon cream dressing—mix ½ cup heavy sweet cream with 1 tablespoon lemon juice and 1 teaspoon grated lemon peel—no other seasoning
Hot biscuits

CHICKEN IN WINE WITH WHITE GRAPES AND ORANGES

Chicken is really a wonderful meat, wonderfully adapted to all cuisines. It is an everyday dish and, despite its modest price, it is still a festive dish. This is for a night when you want your family to feel very, very special. It is also a good party dish.

1 chicken (2½ to 3 pounds), cut up for frying	2 cups chicken broth plus juice of ½ lemon
3 tablespoons butter	2 oranges, peeled and cut into segments
1 tablespoon Curaçao	
1 cup or 1 can white grapes	or
2 cups white wine	1 can mandarin oranges,
or	drained

Sauté the chicken in the butter and brown on both sides. Transfer to a casserole. Add the wine or broth and lemon juice, Curaçao, the grapes, and the orange sections. Bake in a 350° oven 45–50 minutes or until the chicken is tender and the wine sauce has been reduced. Serves 4.

S E R V E   W I T H

> Rice cooked in chicken broth
> Lettuce, water cress and endive, with French dressing
> Hot butterflake rolls

BAKED CHICKEN WITH BLACK WALNUTS

It is best when serving this dish to friends to find out beforehand whether they like black walnuts or are inclined to gastronomic adventure. People with timid and conventional eating habits quite frequently do not care for the entrancing but gamey flavor of black walnuts. The uncooked Irish or Scotch steel-cut oatmeal gives an unusual texture and interesting flavor to the chicken.

1 large fryer (about 3–3½ pounds), cut in pieces
1 cup Irish oatmeal (uncooked)
Salt, pepper, margarine
½ cup finely chopped black walnuts
2 eggs, slightly beaten
½ cup salad oil or peanut oil

Pat the chicken dry. Mix the oatmeal, seasoning, and black walnuts, and put into a paper bag. Dip the chicken pieces one at a time into the slightly beaten egg, and then shake in the paper bag with the oatmeal and nut mixture until well coated. Brown the chicken on all sides in the shortening and arrange in a shallow casserole. Bake in a 325° oven for 45–50 minutes or until chicken is fork-tender. Serves 4.

SERVE WITH

Spoonbread (p. 191)
Green peppers and sour cream

MARYLAND FRIED CHICKEN WITH CREAM GRAVY

The favorite way of cooking and eating chicken according to many surveys is fried. Some rather dubious ways of frying are labeled "southern" presumably to make it sound glamorous. One of the best of the southern ways, to my way of thinking, is the batter-fried chicken served in Maryland with a cream gravy, corn fritters, and ham or crisp bacon curls.

2 teaspoons salt	2 cups half milk, half cream
½ teaspoon pepper	Salt and pepper
1 cup flour	1 tablespoon finely chopped
1 large broiler-fryer chicken,	chives
cut up for frying	1 tablespoon finely chopped
2 eggs, beaten	parsley
4 slices lean pork	

Mix the salt, pepper, and cup of flour in a paper bag. Dip the pieces of chicken into it, one or two at a time, shaking around in the bag until well floured. Dip into beaten egg and then back into the flour. Flour lightly the slices of salt pork. Sauté the pork in a heavy skillet until lightly browned on all sides. Remove and keep warm. Pour off some of the fat into a container and sauté the pieces of chicken in the skillet in the remaining fat. Turn heat low and cook until fork tender and no pink shows, about 35–40 minutes. Remove chicken to warm platter with the salt pork. Take a little of the seasoned flour, about ¼ cup, and add enough of the reserved fat to make approximately ¼ cup, but just guess, don't measure. Stir together over low heat until slightly browned. Add the milk and cream, gradually, stirring until thick and smooth. Season with salt and pepper to taste, add the chives and parsley. Serve the gravy in a fat pitcher. Serves 4.

SERVE WITH

> Corn fritters
> Ham or Canadian bacon curls
> Fried tomato slices
> Biscuits

DICED CHICKEN WITH SHRIMP SAUCE AND BACON RICE

This dish, which may use any diced cooked chicken, is particularly good when made with chicken that has been cooked on a rotisserie, whether done at home or brought from the market.

3 cups diced cooked chicken
1 can frozen condensed cream of shrimp soup
½ cup light cream or more calorically, heavy cream
1 jigger sherry

More cooked shrimp (not necessary but a nice, generous touch—if canned ones are used, rinse in cold water, remove black vein)

Bacon Rice

1½ cups raw rice
3 cups chicken broth or chicken bouillon cubes and 3 cups water

3 spring onions, tops and bottoms chopped
4 slices cooked crumbled bacon

Heat the chicken in the frozen shrimp soup with the cream, sherry, and extra shrimp, if you are using them. Check the seasonings and add more salt, if desired. Add a pinch only of tarragon and a pinch only of grated lemon peel. Put the rice in the pan with the chicken broth and spring onions. Bring to a boil, cover, and turn the heat down very low for 15–20 minutes. Remove the lid and fluff the rice with a fork. Add the crumbled cooked bacon and put into a serving dish. Serves 4.

SERVE WITH

Lettuce, cooked cold Italian green beans, chopped parsley, and French dressing
Hot biscuits

VIRGINIA FRIED CHICKEN

Despite the fact that fried chicken is supposed to be the preferred way of cooking it, it's one of the most difficult things for most people to cook well. At the Delmarva Chicken Festival, where some very, very peculiar ingredients are used by contestants trying to be different and capture the prize, top honors went one year to an older woman who merely fried the chicken this way (more or less).

1 chicken, 2½–3 pounds, cut up for frying
1 pint buttermilk
Flour

Salt and pepper
3 tablespoons butter
3 tablespoons cooking oil

Skin the pieces of chicken and soak in the buttermilk for about an hour. Remove them one by one, and shake them in a paper bag with flour, salt, and pepper to flour them thoroughly and remove. Heat butter and oil, and sauté pieces of chicken until a golden brown on all sides. Drain and serve. Serves 4.

SERVE WITH

>   Fresh or frozen asparagus
>   Cole slaw
>   Spoonbread (p. 191)

CHICKEN WITH YOGURT SAUCE

All the delicately acid and lovely variations of milk, sour cream, yogurt and buttermilk have a gentling effect on the chicken or meat that they are cooked with, seeming to tenderize while subtly complementing the flavors.

1 chicken (2½–3 pounds), cut up for frying	1 cup yogurt
2 medium-sized onions, chopped	1 teaspoon grated lemon peel
3 tablespoons butter	Salt and pepper
1 tablespoon flour	Mashed potatoes
	Walnut halves

Sauté the chicken in butter until golden brown, being careful not to burn. Add onions, salt and pepper, and 1 cup of water. Cover tightly and simmer over low heat until tender, about 25–30 minutes. Mix the flour with the yogurt and lemon peel and pour over the chicken. Stir well until this mixture is smoothly mixed with the juices from the chicken. Simmer about 10 minutes more and serve. Serve on hot platter surrounded with a ring of mashed potatoes. Arrange walnut halves at decorative intervals on the mashed potatoes. Serves 4.

SERVE WITH

Whole, baked tomatoes (p. 132)
Blueberry muffins

ARROZ CON POLLO

Chicken with rice is cooked in many different ways in many different countries, and this is indeed not according to strict Spanish rules. It is a Balkan version which somehow retained the Spanish name.

2–2½ cups diced uncooked chicken (chicken weighing about 3–3½ pounds)
¼ cup butter (½ stick)
1 cup raw rice or 1 package yellow rice
1 medium-sized onion, chopped fine
1 clove garlic
1 can (No. 2½) tomatoes,
     or
5 large fresh ones, diced and seeded

Chicken broth (there must be 3 cups liquid, which may include that from the canned tomatoes)
¼ teaspoon thyme
½ cup coarsely chopped walnuts
Salt and pepper

Sauté the rice and onion and garlic in the butter until lightly colored. Add the diced chicken and sauté slightly. Turn into a shallow large baking dish that comes to the table. Add the tomatoes, broth, thyme, salt, and pepper. Sprinkle the top with the walnuts. Put in a 350° oven and bake 35–45 minutes, until the rice is cooked and most of the liquid has been absorbed. Serves 4.

SERVE WITH

Fresh asparagus
Sesame seed rolls

PAN-BROILED CHICKEN BREASTS
WITH SPINACH SOUFFLÉ

Chicken breasts, skinned and basted with a stick of butter, two table-spoons of vinegar (preferably tarragon), and a teaspoon of dry English mustard, pan-broiled until tender and lightly browned, then sprinkled with slivered almonds, seem to embellish the most simple meal. Unless some unforeseen disaster overtakes our poultry flocks in the near future, it will also remain inexpensive. Someone is always being tiresome about spinach. Either you should eat it because it is good for you or you shouldn't because it is bad for you. No one seems to care how *good* it tastes when properly cooked and seasoned.

Spinach Soufflé

3 tablespoons butter	⅛ teaspoon nutmeg, *no more*
3 tablespoons flour	Salt and pepper
1 cup milk	3 eggs, separated
⅓ cup freshly grated Parmesan cheese	1 package frozen chopped spinach

Melt the butter, add the flour, and cook a few minutes before stirring in the milk, slowly, cooking until smooth and thickened. Remove from the fire and add the seasonings and egg yolks, and blend well. Add the partially or wholly thawed chopped spinach. Whip the egg whites until stiff and fold in gently with a rubber spatula. Turn into a greased casserole with straight sides. Bake in a 350° oven 50 minutes or more or until the top springs back when lightly touched. Serves 4.

SERVE WITH

Chicken breasts
Tiny new potatoes, boiled and served in their skins with butter and sour cream

CHICKEN AND CHESTNUT CASSEROLE

Cook books say to notch chestnuts with crosses and then drop them in boiling water or roast them but never, never, how difficult it is or how tough the chestnuts. The easiest thing to do if you cannot buy the already roasted ones from a street vendor is to get the dried Italian ones. Treat them like dried legumes. Soak them first for a long period (overnight or 48 hours), then simmer until tender.

1 roast chicken (roasted in oven at 350° until tender) or rotisserie chicken, 3–3½ pounds
¼ pound butter
2 tablespoons sugar
1 pound small white onions, peeled and parboiled,
   or
1 can onions, drained

1 can Belgian baby carrots
½ pound chipolata or bratwurst, cut in pieces
¾ pound dried chestnuts, soaked and then cooked in consommé
¼ pound diced bacon, cooked until crisp

Place the roast chicken in a casserole or on a hot platter. Glaze the onions and the carrots, heating first in the butter and then adding the sugar. Surround the chicken with the vegetables and the chipolata or bratwurst, sprinkle the chestnuts and the cooked bacon over all. This is a dry casserole and has no gravy. Serve with coarse salt crystals. Serves 4 to 6.

SERVE WITH

Leaf lettuce with lemon dressing (p. 107)
French bread

POULET PICASSO

This is said to be the way Picasso prefers his chicken, or at least as one restaurant says that he does. It is much like any other chicken that is broiled and basted with olive oil, and then served in a tomato sauce. The magic ingredient seems to be the 20 pitted large ripe olives, and 20 pitted large green olives. Of course, olives do turn up, from time to time, in other chicken and tomato dishes such as the Puerto Rican Chicken Asopoa on page 127.

1 chicken, 2½–3 pounds, split, flattened and quartered (the original version calls for ½ a chicken for each person)
⅓ cup olive oil
¼ cup slightly melted butter

4 large ripe tomatoes, peeled, quartered, and seeded
20 large ripe olives and 20 large green olives, pitted
Salt and pepper

Salt and pepper the chicken, place in a shallow baking dish, and drizzle with the oil. Bake uncovered in a 400° oven for about 25 minutes, basting from time to time with the olive oil and juices in the pan. Remove and transfer to a warm platter. Pour the melted butter over it. Meanwhile, cook the tomatoes in their juices for 4 or 5 minutes. Add the olives and pour over the chicken pieces. Serves 4.

S E R V E   W I T H

Parched rice (white rice that has been toasted dry in a skillet until nicely browned, and then cooked in the usual way with chicken broth 15–20 minutes)
Curly endive with blue cheese dressing
Hard rolls

SOUTH AFRICAN CHICKEN PIE

It is true that frozen chicken pie, a boon to harried mothers, can be found in every grocery, but there are wonderfully varied and savory versions to be made with just a little time, and tender loving care.

1 chicken, 2½–3 pounds	1½ tablespoons cornstarch
10 small white onions	3 tablespoons lemon juice
4 whole allspice	1 egg yolk, slightly beaten
1 cup white wine	2 hard-cooked eggs, sliced
¼ teaspoon nutmeg	¼ pound diced cooked or un-
12 peppercorns	cooked ham
3 tablespoons butter	pastry for top of pie

In the original version the chicken was cooked with the bone in but, for convenience in eating, pull the meat from the carcass before cooking and cut into bite-size pieces. Put in a shallow casserole that will take top-of-stove heat the pieces of chicken with the onions, allspice, white wine, 2 cups of water, nutmeg, and peppercorns. Simmer, covered, for about 20 minutes until the chicken and the onions are partially done and the liquid slightly reduced. Remove the peppercorns and allspice. Add the sliced hard-cooked eggs and diced ham. Cook remaining liquid with butter and cornstarch mixed with the lemon juice until slightly thickened over low heat. Remove from the fire and add a little of the hot liquid to the slightly beaten egg yolk. Blend well with the rest of the thickened liquid and pour over the ingredients in the pie dish. Top with the pastry and bake in a 350° oven for 45 minutes. Serves 4 to 6.

SERVE WITH

Bowl of plain water cress
Biscuits

A RING MOLD OF CURRIED CHICKEN WITH
WHITE GRAPES AND KUMQUATS

It's a very odd household in these days of poultry plenty that doesn't have chicken or turkey once or twice a week. It is one of the most adaptable of meats, and still has a party air despite its modest price.

3 cups diced cooked chicken, preferably home-roasted, or from a nearby rotisserie
½ cup fresh or canned (and drained) white grapes
⅓ cup diced preserved kumquats (remove the inner structure)

1 can chicken curry soup
 or
1 can undiluted condensed cream of celery soup
1½ tablespoons Madras curry powder
2 eggs

Mix the diced cooked chicken with the white grapes, kumquats, and the soup or sauce that has been mixed with the eggs in a blender, if you have one; if not, beat the eggs with a rotary beater before adding them to the soup or sauce. Turn the mixture into a buttered ring mold, about quart size, and set the ring mold in a pan holding about an inch of water. Put in a 350° oven for about 45–50 minutes, or until a knife inserted comes out clean. Remove and unmold on a warm round platter. Surround with yellow rice, cooked according to the directions on the package. Fill the center with diced spiced peaches or pears. Serves 4 to 6.

SERVE WITH

Fresh peas or asparagus
Hot cloverleaf rolls

GRILLED CHICKEN WITH HOME-MADE NOODLES

Prepare the chicken for grilling by dropping the chicken quarters in boiling water and letting them stand off the heat for 5 minutes. Then drain and pat dry, and cover each part with finely chopped onion mixed with butter. Grill or pan-roast in the oven until tender. Home-made noodles, which taste very, very different from the ready-made ones, are not at all difficult to make. It is possible to get the knack in one or two tries.

Home-made Noodles

1½ cups all-purpose flour, measured before sifting	½ teaspoon salt
2 medium-sized eggs	2–3 drops yellow coloring

Mix the ingredients together with a wooden spoon or your fingers, and let stand before and after rolling. Roll out very thin and cut into strips the width you prefer. Some like the wide ones. I prefer ones about ¼ inch wide. Let them hang to dry on the edge of the work table. To cook, immerse in a large pot of furiously boiling salted water. Cook until barely tender. Test by pinching with your fingers. Drain and dress with 1 stick unsalted butter, melted and heated with 1½ tablespoons chopped parsley, 2 cloves finely chopped garlic, and 1 tablespoon grated lemon peel. Serves 4 to 6.

Broccoli Aspic

1 envelope unflavored gelatin	3 hard-cooked eggs, sliced
1 can condensed consommé	Juice of 1½ lemons
Very little salt and pepper	2 cups cooked broccoli
¾ cup mayonnaise	flowerets

Soften gelatin in ¼ cup of the cold consommé. Add to the rest of the consommé and heat and stir until dissolved, add salt and pepper—cautiously. Let thicken until the consistency of uncooked egg whites, fold in mayonnaise, sliced eggs, cooked broccoli, and lemon juice. Pour into molds or paper cups and chill until firm. This quantity will serve 6.

S E R V E   W I T H

Broccoli in aspic

LEMON CHICKEN

Many barbecue sauces are very, very complicated. One of the simplest and the best is butter and lemon juice with a dash of Tabasco sauce, salt, and pepper. So that the chicken stays juicy during the brief broiling and yet is thoroughly cooked, drop the chicken quarters in boiling water and let stand for 5 minutes. This is an old and valuable Chinese trick.

1 chicken, about 3 pounds, quartered
½ cup melted butter (1 stick)

⅓ cup lemon juice
3–4 drops Tabasco sauce
Salt

Drop the chicken quarters in boiling water and let stand away from the heat for 5 minutes. Pat dry. Mix the butter, lemon juice, and Tabasco, adding it very, very cautiously, and the salt. Arrange the chicken quarters on a broiler, baste the chicken halves with the butter, lemon juice, and Tabasco mixture, using a bulb baster, and broil on both sides until golden brown and fork tender. Serves 4.

S E R V E   W I T H

Kasha pilaf
Creamed spinach
Diced cucumber, peeled, chopped fresh mint with yogurt

CHICKEN ROLLS

The ingredients in this recipe may be varied. Turkey may be used instead of the chicken, or with the chicken instead of the ham. Because whole chicken breasts are used, one is a fairly ample serving for moderate eaters.

4 slices of good country ham
    or
8 slices Canadian bacon
    or
1 jar of Smithfield ham spread

4 whole breasts of chicken, boned
4 slices Swiss cheese or cheddar (no processed cheese)

Place a piece of ham or two pieces of Canadian bacon on each chicken breast, or spread with Smithfield ham spread. Lay a slice of cheese on top of the ham. Roll the chicken, ham, and cheese together, tuck in the edges, and place in a shallow buttered casserole. Dot the top with more butter and sprinkle with Beau Monde seasoning. Bake in a 350° oven about 1 hour, or until fork tender. Serves 4.

S E R V E   W I T H

    Italian salad (p. 39)
    French bread

BREADED CHICKEN BREASTS

Any recipe that calls for chicken breasts, which I prefer, may, of course, use chicken legs or second joints, or a whole chicken may be used if slightly more cooking time is allowed.

8 (halves) chicken breasts
2 eggs
¼ cup fine bread crumbs
(either put into an electric
blender or roll fine with a
rolling pin)
Salt
⅓ cup honey

Dry the chicken pieces thoroughly with paper toweling. Beat the eggs with about 2 tablespoons of water, the fine bread crumbs, and salt. The mixture should be somewhat like thick gravy. The proportions, however, will vary slightly with the size of the eggs. With a pastry brush or, for that matter, a new 25-cent paint brush, brush the chicken pieces with honey on both sides, then dip into the egg and bread crumb mixture, coating thoroughly. Arrange in a shallow, decorative baking dish. Bake at 325° for about 1 hour or until fork tender. Serves 4.

S E R V E   W I T H

Barley pilaf (p. 209)
Garden leaf lettuce sprinkled with fresh lime juice and salt only
Euphrates bread

STUFFED CHICKEN BREASTS I

Chicken breasts that are to be stuffed should be boned either by you or the butcher. It is a reasonably simple process even when done at home. And of course when they are boned, they are also skinned. The whole breast is more manageable for stuffing.

4 whole boned breasts of chicken
2 cups cooked kasha
    or
1 can (15 ounce) cooked kasha

½ cup sliced water chestnuts
½ cup pecans, broken
¼ cup shortening
1 cup chicken broth
. Salt and pepper (the broth has some)

Mix the kasha, water chestnuts, and pecans and put ¼ of the mixture on each chicken breast. Fold each over into a tidy package and skewer with toothpicks or poultry nails. Brown in shortening in a skillet on all sides. Place in a shallow casserole to fit. Add broth, salt, and pepper. Bake at 325° for 1 hour or until fork-tender. Serves 4.

SERVE WITH

Italian green beans
Cherry or yellow pear tomatoes

STUFFED CHICKEN BREASTS II

A different and festive version that is served at the Russian Tea Room in New York and is worthy of that overworked adjective—glamourous.

4 large breasts of chicken (2 whole breasts, split)	4 tablespoons sweet butter (½ stick)
2 chicken legs	Salt and pepper
1 egg	Flour and bread crumbs

Skin the breasts, carefully remove the bones, and pound very thin as for veal scalloppini, between two pieces of waxed paper. Remove the skin from the two legs and cut the meat from the bone and dice. Put the diced leg meat in a blender with half of the butter, salt, and pepper, or put the leg meat through a meat grinder and then mix with half of the butter. Divide into four parts and mold each part with your fingers into about a two-inch-long slender sausage. Wrap each breast around one of these, tucking the ends in, and skewer closed with poultry nails or toothpicks. Roll each stuffed chicken breast in the flour and then in the egg beaten with 2 tablespoons of cold water, and then again in the bread crumbs, making sure each piece is very well covered. Chill for several hours before sautéeing if time permits. Brown in a frying pan in the rest of the sweet butter, then place in a 350° oven for 15 minutes. Serves 4.

SERVE WITH

> Rice cooked in chicken broth with white raisins, slivered almonds, and a dab of butter
> Belgian endive dressed with fresh lime juice and a little salt

BAKED CHICKEN PANCAKES MORNAY

It is only in America that pancakes are for breakfast, with syrup or sausage. Elsewhere, they are main dishes, desserts, hors d'oeuvres— in fact, anything but a breakfast dish. One of the most delightful of the hot hors d'oeuvres is tiny Russian buckwheat blini with melted butter, sour cream, and caviar, either red or black. And of course, the all-purpose Mexican tortilla is nothing but a rather robust pancake made of corn meal, sometimes the blue type, with hot and heavy embellishments. This is one of the more elegant ways of presenting creamed chicken.

Pancakes

1½ cups sifted flour	3 eggs, well beaten
1 teaspoon salt	1½ cups milk

Mix flour and salt, add eggs and milk gradually, stirring until smooth. This may be done in one fell swoop in the blender. If possible, let the batter "rest" for an hour or two before making the pancakes. Bake pancakes, one at a time, in a greased 6½-inch skillet, turning once. Use about ¼ cup batter per pancake, and tilt skillet as you pour in batter so that bottom of skillet is completely covered. Stack cooked pancakes on a plate and keep warm.

Filling

2 cups diced, cooked, or rotisserie chicken	Salt and pepper to taste
1 cup chopped canned or sautéed fresh mushrooms	

Mix the ingredients.

½ cup butter (chicken fat
tastes heavenly)
⅔ cup flour
3 cups chicken stock (canned
or bouillon-cube broth may
be used)
2 cups rich milk
½ cup sauterne or other white
dinner wine

½ cup grated Parmesan or Romano cheese
½ teaspoon Worcestershire
sauce
Dash of mace
Salt and pepper to taste

Melt butter and stir in flour; add chicken stock and milk gradually.
Cook until mixture boils and thickens, stirring constantly. Remove
from heat. Add wine, one-half the cheese, and the seasonings. Place
a spoonful of the chicken-mushroom mixture on each pancake. Roll
up and place side by side in 2 buttered shallow baking dishes (12 x 8
x 2 inches). Pour sauce over pancakes. Sprinkle the rest of the grated
Parmesan cheese over each casserole and dust with paprika. Bake in
a moderately hot oven (375°F.) for about 25 minutes, or until brown
and bubbly. Serve from the baking dishes. These may be prepared
ahead and baked just before serving. Serves 4—allowing three pancakes per person.

SERVE WITH

Spinach and tomato salad—raw spinach torn into pieces and
cherry tomatoes cut in half, tossed with French dressing just
before serving
French bread

CHICKEN OR TURKEY SHORTCAKE

Luckily, in these days of poultry plenty, there is no end to the ways in which cooked chicken or turkey or duck can be used.

2 cups diced cooked chicken or turkey
¼ pound sliced fresh mushrooms
3 tablespoons butter
3 tablespoons flour
1 cup chicken broth

½ cup heavy sweet or sour cream
1 jigger whiskey or sherry
4 toasted corn cakes or corn toast (bought in packages like English muffins)

Sauté the mushrooms in the butter. Remove and sprinkle butter with the flour, and cook until almost dry. (This is the minor point in which most fail in making sauces.) Add broth, a little at a time, stirring constantly until smooth and thickened. Add the sweet cream and cook until that is thickened. If using the sour cream, it must be added just before removing from the stove and not allowed to come to a boil. Add sherry or whiskey, the diced cooked chicken, and cooked mushrooms. Mix and pour between and on top of the split and toasted corn muffin halves. Serves 4.

SERVE WITH

Green peppers baked with onion custard (p. 162)
More corn muffins if desired

CHICKEN ASOPOA

Chicken Asopoa as served in La Mallarquina, in the old part of San Juan in Puerto Rico, is a rather soupy kind of chicken stew. It is especially good when preceded by a couple of ponies of Barralita rum, a honey-smooth liquor, which does not taste like rum, but something more ambrosial.

1 chicken, 2½ to 3 pounds, cut up for frying
3 tablespoons butter
1 cup yellow rice
1 quart chicken broth
1 4-ounce can pimientos, cut in fairly large pieces
1 package frozen asparagus spears
1 package frozen peas
1 small jar green olives, pitted or stuffed
Salt and pepper, if needed

Sauté the chicken briefly until browned on both sides. Transfer to a deep casserole and add the rice, broth, pimientos, asparagus, peas and olives. Cover and cook over low heat about 45 minutes, or until tender. Add salt and pepper if needed. (Some chicken broths are more highly seasoned than others.) Serves 4 to 6, generously.

SERVE WITH

French bread
Candied orange peel and cream cheese

DICED CHICKEN WITH ALMONDS

Chinese dishes have the advantage of being elegant and flavorful and at the same time low in calories and cholesterol. The mixed textures are particularly appealing to American palates.

2 tablespoons cooking oil
1½ teaspoons salt
2 cups diced cooked or uncooked chicken
1 cup diced celery
½ cup sliced water chestnuts
½ cup frozen peas
½ cup bamboo shoots
2 tablespoons cornstarch mixed with ½ cup cold water

½ cup slivered almonds (true Chinese almonds which are a little more bitter than ours are hard to come by, even in Chinatown—peach or apricot kernels, cracked open, have much the same flavor but should be mixed with our milder almonds)

Put the oil in a hot skillet with the salt. Add the chicken and stir well. Then add the celery, water chestnuts, peas and bamboo shoots. Add 1 cup water, cover, and cook for 10 minutes. Add the cornstarch mixture, stir, and sprinkle with the almonds. Serves 4.

SERVE WITH

Rice
Strawberry tarts

129

CREAMED CHICKEN IN PATTY SHELLS

A vol-au-vent, one of the elegant dishes of the Edwardian and Gaslight eras was the *pièce de résistance* at such ceremonious occasions as wedding breakfasts. In the traditional form, an oval puff paste casserole as container with a lid was filled with a sublimated version of creamed chicken and mushrooms and often sweetbreads. Without much practice or expert instruction, puff paste is difficult for a beginner to make. Vol-au-vent crusts may be ordered from fine bakeries, and most of them have on hand patty shells which are miniature (and alas less dramatic) vol-au-vents without lids. The patty shells are also sold frozen. Any can be used with this traditional filling.

½ pound small mushrooms, cut in half
3 tablespoons butter
2 cups diced white meat of boiled or roasted chicken
¼ cup dry sherry
1 cup heavy cream
2 tablespoons Hollandaise sauce (simple to make in a blender but, unless one is a restaurateur, few have 2 tablespoons on hand—it is possible to use the bottled kind obtainable in grocery stores)
4 or 6 patty shells, depending on size

Sauté the mushrooms in the butter for 2 or 3 minutes. Add the diced white meat and cook with the mushrooms for 2–3 minutes more. Add the sherry, let it boil for a minute or two, and turn the heat down. Add the heavy cream and cook over low heat for 10 minutes. Remove from fire, add Hollandaise sauce and turn into warm patty shells. Some of the filling will overflow the shells for 4 servings. There are 6 patty shells in a package of the frozen ones, and this recipe will fill them adequately, if less lavishly.

SERVE WITH

French-cut green beans with toasted slivered almonds

CHICKEN AND ALMOND LOAF

This is an elegant and easy way of using cooked chicken, either roasted or boiled. Canned mushroom soup with a generous dash of sherry will do as a sauce on one of those days when the roof springs a leak or the baby has the measles. On other nights, make your own sauce from fresh or frozen mushrooms.

3 cups finely chopped cooked chicken
½ cup blanched almonds, coarsely chopped or slivered
1 tablespoon finely chopped onion, sautéed in butter
2 cups half-and-half or 1 cup light cream and 1 cup milk

1 cup soft home-made breadcrumbs
2 eggs
½ cup celery, finely chopped
1 cup chicken stock
Salt and pepper

Mix the ingredients, in the order given. Bake in buttered bread pan in 375° oven for 45 minutes. Serve in slices with mushroom sauce or giblet gravy. Serves 4.

Mushroom Sauce

¼ pound mushrooms, sliced through caps and stems
3 tablespoons flour
½ cup cream
2 tablespoons sherry

3 tablespoons butter
1 cup chicken broth
1 teaspoon lemon juice
Salt and pepper

Sauté the mushrooms slowly in the butter until lightly browned. Sprinkle with the flour and cook briefly, stirring well. Add the chicken broth slowly, stirring all the while, and then the cream and the rest of the ingredients. Bring to a boil and serve hot. For another short cut, sautéed mushrooms and sherry may be added to a canned beef gravy.

SERVE WITH

Tiny new potatoes, boiled in their skins
Cold boiled artichokes, with heavily salted and peppered olive
    oil for dipping
Hot biscuits

SIMPLIFIED CHICKEN CURRY WITH NOODLES

Even the most dedicated cook, who prefers to cook from scratch, has some days when there is absolutely no time at all to cook and feed her family and get to some engagement on time.

3 cups diced cooked chicken
    (preferably roasted or from
    a rotisserie)
1 can chicken curry
    soup (Chalet Suzanne)

1 tablespoon curry powder
1 package egg noodles

Heat diced, cooked chicken in the curry soup with extra curry powder. Cook the noodles in boiling, salted water until just barely tender. Drain and put on a heated platter, and pour the chicken and curry soup on top. Serves 4.

SERVE WITH

Asparagus vinaigrette
Spiced peaches or pears or chutney
Hot sesame rolls

GIBLETS WITH ITALIAN GREEN NOODLES

When the dish has not too much color of its own, the green noodles look more appetizing.

1 pound chicken giblets	1 teaspoon grated lemon peel
1 can chicken gravy	1 package Italian green noodles
3 tablespoons white wine	

Trim the giblets of any ragged edges and cut the gizzards into small pieces. Simmer in water to cover about a half hour or until fork-tender. Drain, reduce the cricken broth to about half by cooking, and add the chicken gravy, wine, and lemon peel. Simmer together for a minute or two. Add giblets and cook for a few minutes over low heat. Meanwhile, drop the green noodles into a large pan of salted boiling water, about 3 quarts, and cook until just barely tender. Remove from heat and drain. Put on a hot platter with the giblet mixture poured on top. Serves 4.

SERVE WITH

> Whole baked tomatoes—cut a small piece from the stem-end
> of each tomato, put stem-side down in muffin tin, and bake
> until skin is wrinkled but not broken—10 to 15 minutes
> Bread sticks

NINO'S CHICKEN SALAD

This salad, as served at New York's Drake Hotel, is different from most chicken salads in that it uses cooked vegetables. It is indeed a meal in itself with some crusty French bread, and is equally good with turkey or duck in place of the chicken.

4 cups diced roast chicken or turkey (about 2 small rotisserie-cooked chickens)
2 cups cold cooked green beans
1 cup cold cooked carrots, cut julienne, or 1 can Belgian baby carrots (#1), drained and chilled
2 medium boiled potatoes, sliced

2 medium-sized sliced beets or 1 small can sliced beets, drained
½ cup chopped raw Spanish onion
Chopped fresh parsley (preferably the Italian variety with flat leaves)

Dressing

2 jiggers wine vinegar
2 jiggers olive oil

Salt and pepper
1 drop Maggi sauce

Mix the sauce together and arrange the chilled vegetables and chicken in a bowl or platter. Pour the dressing over, and toss lightly to mix. Serves 4.

SERVE WITH

French bread

Other dishes using chicken:
Sliced Meat Aspic (p. 94)
Pastel de Choclo (p. 32)

CHICKEN LIVERS WITH MADEIRA SAUCE

In this streamlined version, the livers may be fresh or frozen, and of course plain rice may be used instead of the more elegant saffron rice. The Madeira sauce is an involved process when made at home, but the canned Madeira sauce is very good, as is the canned beef gravy with wine added.

1½ pounds chicken livers
  Flour
3 tablespoons butter or bacon drippings

2 cans Leibig's Madeira sauce
  or
1 can beef gravy plus ¼ cup Madeira or red wine

Pimiento Rice

1 10-ounce box yellow rice— seasoned with saffron
2½ cups chicken broth

2 cans whole pimientos, cut in strips
½ small can water chestnuts, drained and sliced thin

Cut chicken livers in half, dust lightly with flour, and sauté briefly in the fat. Add the Madeira sauce or beef gravy with wine, and keep warm. Put the yellow rice and chicken broth in a pan, bring to a broil, cover tightly, and turn the heat down very low. Cook 15–20 minutes without peeking. Remove from the heat and fluff with a fork. Stir in the pimiento strips and water chestnuts. Put chicken livers and sauce in center of a hot platter or shallow casserole. Spoon the rice, pimiento, and water chestnut mixture around the edges. Serves 4.

SERVE WITH

Pimiento rice
Italian green bean salad with finely chopped onion and French dressing
Hot rolls

POLENTA WITH CHICKEN LIVER SAUCE

In the north of Italy, corn meal mush called polenta in Italy and marmalega in Rumania is served with much the same sauces that are used for pasta in the south. The corn meal is ground a bit finer and can be found in most Italian food stores. It is cooked in a huge pot of boiling water with a handful of corn meal thrown in at a time; turn the heat down after each addition, or else it goes plop in your face. It is stirred all the while with a wooden spoon and then poured into some kind of ceramic or pyrex dish or loaf pan that has been well buttered. Chill until firm. To serve, unmold on a platter and cut into slices, holding a piece of string in both hands. This is the traditional manner. You could, of course, be crass and use a knife. It must be layered in a casserole or on a platter and heated before serving.

¾ pound round steak, ground
1 clove garlic, minced
2 medium-sized onions, chopped
2 tablespoons olive oil
1 can tomatoes (#2½), put through sieve

1 can tomato paste
1 teaspoon dried basil or 1 tablespoon chopped fresh basil
1 pound chicken livers, cut in pieces
2 tablespoons butter

Sauté the round steak, garlic, and onions in the olive oil. Add sieved tomatoes, tomato paste, and basil. Simmer 1 hour or more, or even 2–3 hours, adding a can of water from time to time if it needs thinning out. The longer it cooks, the smoother and richer it will be, but a little water must be added from time to time and then cooked down. Just before serving, sauté the lightly floured chicken livers in the butter in a separate skillet, and add to the sauce. Serves 4 to 6.

SERVE WITH

Tossed salad with oil and vinegar dressing, and sliced raw fresh mushrooms
Italian bread sticks

CHICKEN LIVERS WITH CURRIED PILAF

This is a delicious dish, not typical of any one cuisine.

1½ pounds chicken livers
    Flour, salt and pepper
3 tablespoons butter

¼ cup rich chicken broth
¼ cup wine

Dust the livers with flour or shake in a bag with flour and seasonings. Sauté briefly in the butter, add the broth and wine, and simmer while you make the pilaf.

Pilaf

1 cup rice
1 stick butter
2 cups beef bouillon

1 cup tomato purée
1 teaspoon Madras curry
    powder

Cook the rice in the butter slowly, until grains become opaque. Add the stock and the tomato purée and curry powder, and bring to a boil. Cover and turn heat down very low. Cook over low heat for 30–35 minutes or until liquid is absorbed. When rice is cooked in butter first, the cooking time is longer. Serve the chicken livers on top of the pilaf. Serves 4.

SERVE WITH

    Diced green peppers sautéed in oil and served with yogurt
    Armenian bread

CHICKEN LIVERS AND MUSHROOMS

This is a robust Italian way of cooking chicken livers as served at Rose's Restaurant on the west side of midtown New York, much loved by publishing and advertising men nearby.

1¾ pounds chicken livers	1 teaspoon rosemary
¼ pound butter	½ clove garlic, minced fine
⅓ cup finely chopped parsley	Salt and pepper
½ pound fresh mushrooms, sliced	Olive oil
	Flour

Dust the livers lightly with flour. Heat the oil and drop livers in for 5 minutes. Remove and drain. Meanwhile, make a sauce by browning the butter, then sautéeing the garlic and mushrooms. Add the seasoning and the chicken livers and sprinkle with the parsley. Serves 4 hungry men.

SERVE WITH

Parched rice (p. 115)
Leaf lettuce with French dressing
Poppy seed rolls

ROCK CORNISH HENS

There is something very dashing about having a small stuffed bird for each person, and their cost is modest. With this in mind, buy a bird for each person weighing about a pound, or slightly less, rather than the larger ones to be divided in half.

4 Rock Cornish game hens, about 1 pound each
Powdered ginger
Salt and pepper
1 can wild rice stuffing (more frugal than uncooked rice)

3 tablespoons butter
½ can mixed mandarin oranges and pineapple
¼ cup shelled pistachio nuts
8 strips bacon

Rinse the hens under cold running water and dry. Rub them inside and out with powdered ginger, and sprinkle with salt and pepper. Cut the orange segments into small pieces. Mix the canned wild rice stuffing with the drained mandarin oranges and pineapple. Add the pistachio nuts to the mixture. Divide the stuffing and fill the birds, being careful not to pack. Skewer closed and tie the legs together with string. Place the birds, breast side up, on a roasting rack. Cover the breasts with bacon. Roast in an oven preheated to 350° for 40–50 minutes, or until tender. Baste occasionally with drippings in the pan. Serve hot. Serves 4.

Purée of Green Peas

Peas taste well, I think, cooked and served almost any way. Somehow the flavor is different and good when puréed.

1 package frozen peas
½ teaspoon sugar
⅛ teaspoon nutmeg
½ cup light cream

1 cup chopped, raw mushrooms (the stems will do) Salt and freshly ground black pepper

Cook the green peas in water with sugar according to directions on the package. Drain and put into the glass container of an electric blender and add the rest of the ingredients. Blend until well puréed. The peas and the mushrooms may be puréed in a food mill and the rest of the ingredients added. Heat if necessary, but do not let boil. Serves 4.

S E R V E   W I T H

Purée of green peas   Hot butterflake rolls

TURKEY CASSEROLE

Not a tetrazzini but, as they say in the south, kin.

½ pound mushrooms, sliced	1½ cups half cream, half milk
1 small white onion, minced	½ cup white wine
4 tablespoons (½ stick) butter	2–3 cups diced cooked turkey
4 tablespoons flour	1 small jar chopped pimientos
Salt and pepper	1 small can chopped ripe olives (½ cup or half a 4½-ounce can)
1 lump chicken from the dehydrated chicken noodle soup	1 large can Chinese noodles

Sauté the mushrooms and the onions in butter until lightly browned. Sprinkle the flour on top; add the salt and pepper. Stir until blended. Gradually add the half-and-half with the lump of chicken broth, and stir until thickened and smooth. Add the white wine, stir until blended, then add the turkey, pimientos, and ripe olives. Mix together and pour over the noodles in a shallow casserole. Heat briefly and serve. Serves 4.

S E R V E   W I T H

Lemon sherbet, as an accompaniment to the turkey
Mixed frozen vegetables with onion sauce
Toasted English muffins

ROAST TURKEY, CHINESE STYLE

This manner of roasting a turkey takes much less time than the conventional ones, and the bird becomes a beautiful mahogany, full of juice and flavor. Pork loin or a pot roast may be done in the same way. The boiling liquid may be saved, if refrigerated, and used several times. You must have a large, deep roasting pan with a tight cover of enamelware. The size depends upon the size of the turkey you usually roast. A 15–20 pound turkey takes a 20–pound pan, a smaller one a smaller size.

1 turkey, 12–15 pounds	4 large slices fresh ginger or
9 cups water, not including	2 tablespoons chopped pre-
basting	served ginger
3 cups soy sauce	3 scallions
1½ cups sherry	1½ tablespoons salt
2 tablespoons sugar	

Boil the water with the seasonings in a roasting pan on top of the stove. Add the turkey and continue to boil briskly, for 45–50 minutes, turning over from time to time because the juice does not cover the turkey. Remove the juice and put uncovered in a roasting pan. Bake in a 500° oven for 45–50 minutes for a 12–15 pound turkey, basting with juice every 20 minutes and turning over until well browned. Let stand about 10 minutes or so before serving and carving. Store the juice or liquid in containers in the refrigerator. A 5-pound chicken needs only 15 minutes' boiling, 20 minutes' steeping in the liquid, and 15 minutes' basting and browning in a very hot oven, and, of course, less ingredients (3 cups water, 1 cup soy sauce, 1 tablespoon sugar, ½ cup sherry, ¾ slices fresh ginger, and 1 scallion) and also a smaller pan.

Flaming Cranberries

Cook 3 cups of fresh cranberries in a baking dish or a stove-to-table skillet dish with 1 cup of honey and 1 cup of hot water, a tablespoon of grated lemon peel and a tablespoon of grated orange peel. Cover and bake in a 375° oven for about 1 hour or until the skins pop. Serve hot with the turkey. Pour over ½ cup of warmed brandy, light, and bask in the cheerful glow.

Flaming cranberries
Corn-bread stuffing, baked separately—2 batches corn bread,
  broken up and mixed with chopped raw onion, chopped raw
  celery, eggs, and chicken broth
Assorted relishes, ripe and green olives, and celery stalks

CREAMED TURKEY HASH

In the olden days, when one generally had turkey only for Thanks-
giving and Christmas or other momentous occasions, it seemed almost
a desecration to make the turkey that was left into hash. It tasted so
wonderfully good when picked from the bones the next day. Now,
when anyone can have turkey once a week, this very special kind of
hash, which is in fact diced turkey in a fine cream sauce, is a goodly
dish. Especially is this true when served in a ring of rice cooked in
cranberry juice, with possibly some pineapple chunks and pieces of
crystallized ginger added.

4 tablespoons butter	Salt and pepper
4 tablespoons flour	2 cups diced cooked turkey
2 cups half-and-half or light cream	2 tablespoons sherry

Make a cream sauce by melting the butter, adding the flour, and cooking slightly before adding the cream slowly. Stir constantly while cooking over low heat, until smooth and thickened. Add salt and pepper,
turkey and sherry. Heat thoroughly. This may be made ahead of time
and kept warm in a double boiler. Serves 4.

SERVE WITH

Rice (see above)
Onion and apple casserole (p. 202)
Butterflake rolls

ROAST BABY TURKEY, UNSTUFFED

This is a menu which may be quickly adapted to the abrupt changes that sometimes occur in our weather. Serve it hot with the sweet potatoes or cold with fruit salad.

Sprinkle the unstuffed bird inside with salt. Tie the legs and tail together neatly. Brush all over lightly with melted fat. Place on rack in shallow covered pan. Roast at 350°, basting once or twice with melted fat or pan drippings. Use whatever fat you prefer. My preference is for butter, bacon drippings or, best of all, the chicken fat available rendered in most delicatessens. A 4 pound, ready-to-cook weight turkey roasted unstuffed will take about 2 hours. One of 4–8 pounds, ready-to-cook weight, will take about 3 hours. When done, the leg joints should move easily, and when pricked with a fork, the juice coming out should be clear. Let the turkey "rest" 15–30 minutes before carving. This makes the carving easier.

Baked Stuffed Sweet Potatoes

Scrub the skins of the sweet potatoes and butter them thoroughly. Bake in a 350° oven until done, about an hour or more depending upon size. When done, let cook for easier handling. Cut in half and remove carefully from the skins without tearing. Mash and mix with the apricot and horse-radish sauce. Pile lightly into the skins. This may be done earlier in the day or even the day before. To serve, bake for about 30 minutes at 350° or until piping hot.

SERVE WITH

> Baked sweet potatoes with apricot-horse-radish dressing (p. 77)
> or Water cress, grapefruit, white grape salad with French dressing
> Hot biscuits

ROAST DUCK, UNSTUFFED, WITH
STUFFED PRUNES AND BACON

Roast the duck unstuffed but rubbed inside and out with powdered ginger, and sprinkle with salt and pepper according to the directions given on page 146 for Roast Duck with Greek Stuffing. Fill prunes which have been soaked overnight and then drained and pitted with softened cream cheese mixed with horse-radish. Skewer a half slice of bacon around each prune with a toothpick and surround roast duck with them for the last 15 minutes of cooking.

French Fried Eggplant

1 medium-sized eggplant
Flour
Salt and pepper

½ teaspoon dried basil
Fat for frying

Peel and cut the eggplant in fingers like potatoes for French fries. Cook in slightly salted water about 10 minutes. Drain and pat dry. Flour the pieces by shaking a few at a time in a paper bag with some flour, salt, pepper and basil. Drop into 380° fat a few at a time and fry until light brown. Sprinkle lightly with more salt. Serve hot. Serves 4.

S E R V E   W I T H

> French fried eggplant
> Pickled celery root—bought in jars
> Brown-and-serve party rolls

ROAST DUCK WITH FRUIT GARNISH

Ducks are everywhere and modest in price although there is not as much edible meat per pound as in chicken.

5 pound duckling, ready for oven	2 tablespoons butter
1 tablespoon curry powder	1 cup white wine
1 clove garlic, finely chopped	Salt and pepper

Garnish

Bananas, peaches, pineapples, pears	Catsup
	Slivered almonds

Rub the duck with the curry and the garlic which is mixed with the butter. It is true that ducks have a lot of fat of their own, but this gives a nice glaze. Sprinkle the cavity with salt and pepper, and put in roasting pan. Put on an ovenrack preheated to 350° and roast for 1–1¼ hours, basting with the wine from time to time. Dice or cube the fruits which may be any seasonable combination. Mix them with a little catsup for color and flavor, and sprinkle the top with slivered almonds. Serve in a small bowl. Let the duck stand a few minutes before carving. Serves 4.

S E R V E   W I T H

> Kasha pilaf
> Armenian bread

DUCK CURRY

Because there is a large amount of waste to a duck, it is not as frugal to use as chicken or turkey, but it is a nice change from time to time.

1 Long Island duckling, 5–6 pounds, dressed weight
2 teaspoons Worcestershire sauce
1 tablespoon Madras curry
Salt and pepper

¼ cup duck fat
1 clove garlic
½ cup finely chopped onion
1½ cups duck broth
¼ cup flour

Cut duck in serving-size pieces, discarding backbone, neck, wing tips, and skin. If the duck is frozen, you will have to thaw sufficiently for the rigor mortis to pass before cutting. Cook the discarded pieces and the giblets in 3 cups of boiling salted water for about 45 minutes. Strain the broth and chill until the fat rises to the top. Lift it off carefully and save. Chop the neck meat and giblets. Rub the pieces of duck with Worcestershire sauce, curry powder, salt, and pepper. Heat the duck fat in a Dutch oven over medium heat. Add the pieces of duck and brown lightly on both sides. Add the garlic and onion and cook for about 2 minutes. Add ¾ cup of duck broth, cover tightly, and cook over low heat until duck is tender, about 45 minutes. Mix the remaining duck broth and flour, add to the pot, and cook until the sauce thickens, stirring constantly. Serve over the rice. Serves 4. Save the remaining broth and giblets for a soup.

SERVE WITH

Rice, cooked in chicken broth
Chutney or, for an economical change, cooked rhubarb, slivered almonds, chopped green pepper, and coconut

ROAST DUCK WITH GREEK DRESSING

As far as I know, there are no ducks or, if so, very few, in the Near East. But this dressing that the Greeks use sometimes with chicken goes very well with the sturdy flavor of duck.

1 Long Island duckling, 5–6 pounds, dressed weight	⅓ cup finely chopped parsley
2 pound-cans garbanzos or chick peas, drained	⅓ cup chopped celery
	½ cup olive oil
	¼ cup lemon juice
3 tablespoons butter	1 teaspoon oregano

Pick the duck over carefully and remove any remaining pinfeathers. Sauté the parsley and celery in the butter, and mix well with the drained garbanzos. Stuff the duck with the mixture and skewer closed with poultry nails. Roast duck, breast side up, on rack in shallow pan in slow oven 325° until tender (about 1½–2 hours), basting from time to time with a mixture of the olive oil, lemon juice, and oregano. Serves 4.

SERVE WITH

Rice cooked in chicken broth, with chopped onion and chopped dried apricots
Lemon and orange salad (see p. 205)
French bread

Fish and Seafood

BROILED TUNA STEAK WITH ANCHOVY BUTTER

Almost any fresh or frozen fish steak—salmon, swordfish, or halibut
—tastes equally well cooked this way.

1½ pounds tuna steak or any of the others	2 teaspoons lemon juice
4 tablespoons butter	1 tablespoon finely chopped chives or parsley
2 tablespoons anchovy paste	

Brush the steak lightly with butter on both sides and place under a
broiler 5–10 minutes on each side, or until the flesh is opaque. Or
pan-broil on the top of the stove. Mix the rest of the butter with the
anchovy paste, lemon juice, and chives, and pour on top of the hot
steaks. It is not usually necessary to heat the last butter mixture as
the heat of the fish steaks does that. Serves 4.

SERVE WITH

Barley pilaf (p. 209)
Poppy seed rolls

SALMON CUSTARD WITH TARRAGON
IN CUCUMBER SAUCE

There is an inclination nowadays to take all forms of custard which are not sweet, turn them into a pie crust, and call them a quiche. It is indeed a fine dish, but sometimes it is done so often that you forget how simple and lovely the custard by itself can be. It is even more delicate if steamed a few minutes (very few) in a pressure cooker, though it can, of course, be set in water and baked in an oven.

2 cups flaked cooked salmon (either frozen, simmered briefly until opaque, or the canned—both well drained)
1¼ cups warm milk

3 eggs
1 teaspoon dried tarragon or 2 teaspoons fresh tarragon
Salt and pepper

Beat the eggs, add the warm but not scalded milk, and beat a little more. Add the salmon, tarragon, salt and pepper (this may all be done in one fell swoop in your electric blender). Pour into the inexpensive aluminum swirly molds which will fit into the 4-quart-size pressure cooker, or into separate custard cups which have been brushed thoroughly with salad oil. Cover with pliofilm or aluminum foil and tie with strings. Do not use elastic bands which disintegrate under pressure. Place on rack in pan. Pour ½ cup hot or boiling water in the bottom of the pan. Seal and cook under pressure for 12 minutes. Reduce pressure immediately, unmold, and serve. When individual molds are used, the time is 7 minutes instead of 12. It is best not to try to do two layers at the same time. The top layer is often not done. If it is baked in the oven, place in one large mold or individual molds in a pan of water in an oven pre-heated to 300° and bake for 1 hour or more. The custard is done when a knife inserted comes out clean. Serves 4.

3 tablespoons butter	1 cup half cream, half milk
3 tablespoons flour	⅓ cup chopped cucumber
½ cup chicken broth	

Melt the butter, add the flour, and cook for a minute or two, stirring constantly. Add the broth first, cooking and stirring until smooth and thickened over low heat for 8–10 minutes. Just before serving, add the cucumber. It should not be cooked at all, just warmed.

SERVE WITH

Greek salad (p. 213)
Hot biscuits

SEA SQUAB

People who are a little timid about preparing and eating fish, and who are not even sure they like it, usually enjoy this. It has practically no bones, no pronounced fishy taste, and is usually inexpensive. The pieces look somewhat like chicken legs, though slightly longer, and are dipped in egg and bread crumbs before frying.

1½ pounds sea squab	or bread crumbs mixed with salt,
1 egg, beaten with 2 table-	pepper, grated Parmesan, and
spoons cold water	parsley
⅔ cup seasoned bread crumbs	Oil for frying

Dip the sea squab, which are bought skinned and dressed, into the egg and then into the seasoned crumbs. Let stand on a piece of aluminum foil in the refrigerator for about ½ hour. Heat the fat in a heavy skillet to 370°. Fry, a few at a time, in the fat for 5–8 minutes or until a golden brown. Drain on paper towels. Serve with wedges of lemon. Serves 4.

SERVE WITH

Risi Pisi (p. 91)
Cucumber salad
Warm hard rolls

SOLE en PAPILLOTE

This is a version admittedly adapted to home use and aluminum foil, which is much easier to come by than cooking parchment or the classic New Orleans pompano.

3 tablespoons butter or margarine	½ pound cooked, peeled and cleaned shrimp
3 tablespoons flour	
1 cup milk	¼ pound fresh sliced mushrooms
2 tablespoons sherry	
Salt and paprika	or
8 small or 4 large fillets of flounder or sole	2 cans (3 ounce) broiled-in-butter mushrooms

Make a cream sauce by melting the butter, blending in the flour, and then adding the milk, sherry, and seasonings slowly. Cook a few minutes until thickened. Tear off 4 pieces of aluminum foil about a foot square. On each piece put ¼ of the fish fillets and ¼ of the shrimp. Drain the liquid from the mushrooms and stir in the sauce. Put ¼ of the mushrooms and ¼ of the sauce on each piece, fold up, and pinch tightly together. Place the 4 bags on a cookie sheet and bake in a 425° oven for 40 minutes. To serve, place on the serving plates and snip through the foil, criss cross. Turn back the foil and eat from the silvery dish. Serves 4.

Spring Salad

A good salad to serve with a light meal has a brisk flavor and some substance, such as bacon pieces and chopped hard-cooked eggs well mingled with the greens.

Dandelion greens, when available, or tender young spinach leaves are good in place of the more usual ones. Wash the greens well and pat dry with a clean dish towel. Hard cook 2 or 3 eggs, starting them in cold water, letting them boil 5 minutes, and cooling them in their own water. This way the whites are tenderer. Peel, slice thin, and add to the greens. Meanwhile, fry slowly 2 pieces of bacon cut in pieces about an inch long. Drain and add to the salad. Pour off all but 1 tablespoon hot bacon fat. Mix with it one tablespoon vinegar, salt, pepper, and ½ teaspoon sugar. Pour while still hot over the bacon, eggs, and greens. Serve immediately.

Saffron rice cooked in chicken broth with butter
Spring salad
French bread

SOLE BERCY

This is a simple and elegant way of cooking filet of sole, or for that matter any other fish fillets you can find, either fresh or frozen. For the Bercy part, it is best if you can track down some shallots, the delicate and sophisticated member of the onion family, usually found in this country mostly in the big cities or fancy grocery stores. Naturally, spring onions may be used with a slightly different emphasis.

1 pound fish fillets (sole, red perch)
4 tablespoons butter
Salt and pepper

4 tablespoons finely chopped shallot
4 tablespoons parsley, chopped
⅓ cup white wine or dry vermouth

Simmer the shallot and parsley and wine in a small saucepan 5–7 minutes or until slightly reduced. Arrange the fish fillets in a shallow baking dish and season with salt and pepper. Dot with the butter, pour over the Bercy sauce, and bake in a 325° oven about 5 minutes or until the fish are opaque and flake when touched with a fork. Serves 4.

SERVE WITH

Capellini with walnuts and garlic oil (p. 88)
Water cress salad with orange and grapefruit segments and French dressing
Party rolls

FISH FILLETS WITH MORNAY SAUCE

This sauce adorns almost any bland food, whether it be fish or chicken or eggs. It goes well, for instance, with fish fillets or fish steaks that are in your or your grocer's freezer.

1 pound frozen or fresh fish fillets or steak
1 bottle clam juice or chicken broth
2 tablespoons butter
2 tablespoons flour
½ cup milk
¼ cup freshly grated Parmesan cheese

¼ cup grated Switzerland Swiss cheese
Salt and pepper
½ cup light cream
2 tablespoons red salmon caviar
or
1 tablespoon capers (nice, but not obligatory)

Simmer the fish fillets or steaks in the clam juice or chicken broth until opaque. This will not take long, but will vary according to the variety. Fish needs very, very brief cooking. Make a sauce by melting the butter, blending in the flour, and adding the liquid that the fish was simmered in. Gradually add the milk, stirring constantly until the sauce is thick and smooth. Simmer gently for 5 minutes, stirring occasionally. Then add the cheeses and salt and pepper. Stir until the cheese is melted, add the cream, and heat through. Arrange the fillets or steaks in a shallow come-to-the-table baking dish. Pour in the sauce. Put in an oven pre-heated to 350° for about 15 minutes. Before serving, if you wish, sprinkle the top with the red caviar or the capers. Serves 4.

SERVE WITH

Baked potatoes
Baked carrots
Tomato halves, topped with a tablespoon of mayonnaise mixed with finely chopped onion and parsley on each, and broiled briefly
Salt sticks

PESCADO *en* ESCABECHE

Most Americans, even those who have been blissfully eating raw oysters and even raw steak for years, hear for the first time of eating raw fish with shock. Yet people have been doing it for years in many parts of the world, in Japan, Hawaii and other Pacific islands. In Latin America, the fish *is* briefly cooked before marinating overnight. In Japan and Hawaii the fish is not exactly raw, although it is not cooked on the stove. It is covered with lime juice and the enzymes cook the flesh, or rather act on it, so that it becomes opaque. It is much the same principle as that of meat tenderizers. This is my version of a Puerto Rican dish.

2 pounds swordfish, fresh or frozen	2 tablespoons finely chopped sweet green pepper
3 teaspoons salt	8 bay leaves
½ teaspoon freshly ground black pepper (a couple of twists of the grinder)	½ teaspoon whole allspice
	1½ teaspoons whole black pepper
1 cup olive oil	½ teaspoon salt
¾ cup cider vinegar	1 small clove garlic, minced
¼ cup water	½ cup pitted small green olives
2 tablespoons finely chopped onion	2 dried hot red peppers, crumbled

Cut the fish in serving-size pieces and then slice each piece so none is more than ½ inch thick. Mix the 3 teaspoons of salt with the ground black pepper, and rub half of it into both sides of the pieces of fish. Heat 3 tablespoons of the oil in a skillet, add the fish, and sauté briefly on both sides, adding more oil if necessary. Transfer fish to a refrigerator dish. Place the vinegar, water, onion, bay leaf, and the rest of the ingredients in a saucepan. Heat to the boiling point and boil one minute. Pour over the fish. Add the remaining olive oil and marinate the fish at least 24 hours before serving cold, turning the fish from time to time. This may also be used as an hors d'oeuvre. Serves 4 to 6.

SERVE WITH

Ring mold of spinach (p. 55)   French bread
French fried fingers of eggplant

SALMON WITH LEMON SAUCE

Salmon, either fresh or frozen, does not seem much like the kind in a can, and, naturally, the fresh is better. However, one has to live in the right place for that. It is best broiled and basted with a liquid for 15 minutes or more, or until the fish flakes with a fork.

4 fresh or frozen salmon steaks (about 1 inch thick)	¼ teaspoon dill weed
½ cup white table wine	½ teaspoon dry mustard
¼ cup olive or salad oil	1 lemon, thinly sliced and seeds removed

Arrange the salmon steaks in a shallow baking dish. Mix the seasonings together and pour over them. Arrange the lemon slices on top. Let stand in the juices for 3–4 hours, if possible. This permeates the steak but is not necessary if pressed for time. Remove for the marinade and place the fish steaks on a greased broiler rack and broil carefully until brown on each side. Cook until fork-tender, basting with the marinade from time to time. This should take about 15 minutes. Serves 4.

SERVE WITH

Tiny new potatoes cooked in their skins
Fresh lima beans
Water cress and cucumber salad
French bread

STUFFED BLUEFISH OR SEA BASS

A handsome stuffed fish, if available, makes a delicious and impressive entrée and takes a comparatively brief time to cook.

1 bluefish or sea bass	⅓ cup chopped onions
1 cup (approximately) bread crumbs	2 tablespoons butter
	Olive oil
1½ teaspoons thyme	Thin slices onion
⅓ cup chopped celery	

Sauté the celery and onion in the butter until barely cooked. Mix with the bread crumbs and the thyme. If using prepared stuffing, be careful not to add too much thyme as some varieties have a sufficient amount. Stuff the fish and sew up the cavity, or skewer with poultry nails. Rub well all over with olive oil. Lay in a baking dish, and arrange thin slices of raw onion on top. Bake in a 375° oven 20–25 minutes, or until the fish flakes when picked with a fork. Serves 4.

SERVE WITH

Tiny boiled new potatoes, peeled and rolled in butter and finely chopped parsley
Grapefruit and lettuce salad with French dressing
Pideh—the large, round flat loaves of Armenian bread

BAKED FISH AND BROCCOLI WITH CHEESE SAUCE

Celery root, which is unknown to many Americans, is a delicate, celery-flavored root that is good mashed or puréed and served as a vegetable, or diced and marinated in a French dressing and served as a salad. It is difficult to find except in markets in large cities or pickled in cans. The texture is much more pleasing, I feel, than cooked celery.

2 packages frozen broccoli	1 cup grated cheddar cheese
4 tablespoons butter	¼ cup sherry
4 tablespoons flour	Salt and pepper to taste
1¼ cups whole milk (or half-	2 pounds fish fillets (sole, hali-
½ cup chicken broth	but, salmon, or perch), fro-
and-half)	zen or fresh

Cook broccoli according to directions on package until barely tender but still crisp, and drain thoroughly. Melt the butter and stir in the flour. Add milk or cream and chicken broth, and cook until mixture is smooth and thick, stirring constantly. Add cheese and stir over low heat until melted. Add sherry and seasonings. Arrange broccoli on the bottom of a greased, shallow baking dish—8″x12″x2″ is a good size. Thaw fish fillets and lay over broccoli, cover with sauce, and dust with paprika. Bake in 375° oven for 25 minutes, or until fish flakes when tested with fork. Serves 4.

SERVE WITH

> Salad—celery root, peeled, diced, and cooked until tender. Drain and dress with wine vinegar to moisten. Cool and chill thoroughly. Serve with French dressing, mayonnaise, or, even better, remoulade sauce
> **Sesame seed rolls**

FISH CAKES

Some convenience foods I think are excellent, but having grown up along the Atlantic seaboard, I take a very, very dim view of things called fish sticks. These fish cakes, which may be made with fresh or frozen fish fillets, make a sturdy, lusty version that bears no resemblance to the commercial fish sticks.

1½ pounds raw or frozen fish fillets, thawed and chopped
1 medium-sized onion, chopped
2 raw eggs

3 tablespoons oil
¼ green pepper, chopped
3 tablespoons bread crumbs
Salt and pepper

Mix ingredients, shape into fish cakes, and fry. Serves 4.

Cooking vegetables in milk is more expensive than in water but more rewarding from both a gourmet's and dietician's viewpoint. Even such an aggressive vegetable as cabbage becomes gentle and amenable, especially if shredded and cooked a very short time.

Five-Minute Cabbage

6 cups shredded cabbage
2 tablespoons flour
1½ cups milk

2 tablespoons melted butter
Salt and pepper

Shred cabbage very fine. Heat milk and cook cabbage in it for 2 minutes. Mix flour and butter together and add salt and pepper. Stir into cabbage. Cook rapidly 3 or 4 minutes, stirring the whole time. Serve with the sauce when cooked. Serves 4.

SERVE WITH

Corn muffins—made from scratch, a mix, or frozen

FISH CHOWDER

A rich and savory chowder, colorful with pink shrimp and mussels in their shells shining softly like black opals, is simple enough for new cooks and pretty enough for anyone.

1 package frozen fish fillets, thawed and cut into pieces
2 large onions, peeled and sliced thin
4 slices bacon, cut in small pieces
12 raw mussels, in their shells, well scrubbed
4 medium-sized potatoes, scraped and diced
1 quart milk
12 cooked shrimp
1 bay leaf
Salt and paprika

Put the pieces of fish, onion, potatoes, and bay leaf in a heavy saucepan with the milk. Cook slowly until the potatoes and onions are tender. Fry the bacon until crisp but not hard. Drain on paper towels. Add to the chowder with the shrimp and mussels. Cook until the mussels open. Add salt, paprika, and about 1 tablespoon bacon fat. Serve in large soup plates. Serves 4.

For variety in green salads, try making one of raw spinach. The vegetable so used is quite different from cooked spinach, but just as delicious.

Raw Spinach Salad

½ pound fresh spinach
3 tablespoons olive or salad oil
3 raw carrots, scraped and grated
Salt and pepper

Pull the center leaves from the ½ pound of spinach, wash carefully and thoroughly to remove even the most persistent sand, drain, and very gently pat dry in a clean dishtowel. Add the scraped and grated raw carrots and mix the fluffy, pretty pile lightly with the spinach leaves that have been torn into small pieces by hand. Salt and pepper very heavily the three tablespoons olive or salad oil. Anoint carrots and spinach until every particle glistens. Do not add vinegar, it is too harsh for this delicate, subtle blend of flavors.

SERVE WITH

Raw spinach salad
Toasted crackers—pilot biscuits or "sea toast"

THIS IS A MUDDLE

A muddle is an old Maryland name for a picnic fish dish cooked on the spot, but it can indeed be cooked indoors in a Dutch oven. It is a culinary cousin to pine bark stew. In Maryland it is generally made from rockfish, called rock, but any local fish will do.

1 rock, shad, or pike, cut into pieces	¼ pound salt pork, cut into thin slices
Salt, black and red pepper	1 batch corn bread, baked from a ready-mix

Cut the fish in pieces and cover bottom of Dutch oven, add a layer of salt pork, and season lightly with salt and generously with black and red pepper. Repeat until all ingredients are used. Add just enough water, the old directions say, to make it doubtful if a muddle is a stew or a soup. Cook over low heat for a half hour, then add the corn bread and cook a half hour more. Slices of corn bread are laid on top of the stew, which act as a thickener. Serve in large heavy soup bowls. Unfortunately, the bones in the fish, which give it such good flavor, do present an eating hazard but it would be unauthentic to make this with boneless frozen fish steaks. Serves 4 to 6, amply.

SERVE WITH

Red cabbage slaw with crumbled Roquefort cheese, sour cream and 2 tablespoons lemon juice
More corn bread

AN UNTRADITIONAL BOUILLABAISSE

The French are inclined to sneer at any deviation from the classic form of their dishes, but do they live in the suburbs involved with chauffeuring, P.T.A.s and Cub Scout dens? This easily and quickly assembled fish mélange permits the most harassed to be relaxed and serene. Present it proudly in a tureen and ladle it into deep bowls.

1 pound package frozen fish fillets (haddock, cod, perch, etc.)
1 can frozen cream of shrimp soup
1 large can tomatoes
1 package frozen Chilean langostinos

1 pint fresh or frozen oysters
¼ cup cognac
½ teaspoon dried saffron
1 frozen King crab or 2 bluestone crabs or ½ pound well-scrubbed mussels in their shells

(The last is not obligatory, but a pleasant bit of clutter is expected in any version of this dish.)

Put the fillets, soup, and tomatoes in a pan. Simmer over a low flame about 15 minutes, then add the langostinos, saffron, oysters, and cognac. Cook 5 minutes. Last, add the "clutter," barely warm this, and serve. Serves 4.

SERVE WITH

A ring of tomato aspic, filled with chopped celery and apple
French bread

PINE BARK STEW

Presumably the name of this fish stew, which is usually cooked out-of-doors, refers to the fire material; certainly there is none in the ingredients. This one, in modest home proportions, may be made indoors.

½ pound sliced bacon or ham trimmings
6–7 finely diced potatoes
4 medium-sized onions, chopped fine

1½ pounds flat fish, cut into 1½–2 inch pieces
½ bottle catsup
Salt, pepper, Tabasco sauce, and crumbled, dried red peppers

Cut bacon into small pieces and brown slowly in a large pot or Dutch oven until crisp. Add potatoes and cook until tender, stirring constantly. Add onions when the potatoes are partly tender. Place the fish on top of the potatoes and onions. Cover with water and add the seasonings. Use a long-handled fork for sticking into pot and gently moving mixture to avoid breaking fish. More catsup may be used if desired. Serves 6.

S E R V E   W I T H

Raw vegetable salad
Lots of crusty rolls

SARDINE RABBIT PIE AND STUFFED GREEN
PEPPERS WITH ONION CUSTARD

To make the sardine rabbit pie, start with a baked 9-inch pie shell. Arrange two cans of sardines, drained, on the bottom of the pie shell, and cover with half the Welsh rabbit recipe on page 178. Heat 15–20 minutes and serve.

Green Peppers with Onion Custard

4 large green bell peppers with tops cut off and seeds and white membrane removed	3 egg yolks, slightly beaten
	1½ cups milk
	Salt and pepper to taste
1 medium-sized onion, finely chopped	½ teaspoon Worcestershire sauce

Heat the milk and add to the beaten egg yolks, onion, salt, pepper, and Worcestershire sauce. Pour into the bell peppers and set the peppers in a small baking dish, close enough together so that they will stand up. Pour water into the bottom of the dish until it is ½ inch deep. Bake in 325° oven for about 20 minutes or until custard is done. That will be when a knife inserted comes out clean. Serves 4.

SERVE WITH

Hot biscuits

BROILED LOBSTER TAILS WITH TARRAGON

There is no substitute for a freshly caught Maine or Canadian lobster eaten on location, but the frozen lobster tails are a pleasant and less expensive change to day-in and day-out menus when fresh lobsters are not available. If your family is very large even this is not an economical dish.

4 frozen lobster tails	½ stick butter
3 tablespoons tarragon vinegar,, with the tarragon leaves in it or 1 teaspoon dried tarragon	1 tablespoon chopped chives
	½ teaspoon dry mustard
	Salt and pepper

Remove with scissors the soft part of the lobster tail and slightly hit the hard upper shell with a mallet or cleaver so that it will lie flat. Melt the butter and add the vinegar, chives and seasonings. Spoon generously over the lobster tails and let stand in the marinade for several hours. Broil about 10–15 minutes (depending on size) with meaty side up, basting from time to time, with the liquid in the pan. Broil about 4 inches from the heat. Serves 4.

SERVE WITH

> Fresh or frozen asparagus
> Water cress and endive salad
> French bread
> Lemon custard

SEAFOOD NEWBURG

Serve the Newburg in a toasted bread case as described below or in the excellent frozen patty shells available almost everywhere.

4 tablespoons butter	3 egg yolks
3 cups cooked seafood (shrimp, crab flakes, mussels, oysters, etc.)	1 cup light cream and ½ cup milk or 1½ cups half-and-half
1 teaspoon paprika, special kind	1 teaspoon salt
½ teaspoon nutmeg	¼ cup sherry
2 tablespoons flour	1 loaf unsliced bread
	¼ cup melted butter

Melt the four tablespoons butter in a heavy skillet (enameled cookware), and flour, stir 2–3 minutes over low heat but do not brown. Add sea food, paprika, nutmeg, and stir in. Beat the egg yolks with milk and cream, add to mixture slowly and cook over low heat—stir with wooden spoon until thickened, but do not boil. Add salt and wine slowly so it will not curdle. Meanwhile, with a sharp knife cut off top of loaf of bread and outside crust. Cut the inside in a box fashion without cutting through, leaving walls about ½ or ¾ inch thick. Brush inside and out with melted butter. Bake in 450° oven 10–15 minutes, or until brown. Fill with hot Newburg and serve at once. Serves 4 to 6.

SERVE WITH

Creamed spinach
Bibb lettuce, white grapes, and sliced avocado with French dressing

A RING OF FLUFFY SPOONBREAD
WITH SHRIMP SAUCE

There are two kinds of spoonbread in the South, the plain kind and the fluffy kind in which the egg whites are beaten separately and folded in just before baking. People elsewhere insist on calling this a spoonbread soufflé but many southerners who would be frightened at making a soufflé make this all the time. It is, of course, the same.

1 cup white cornmeal
1 teaspoon salt
1 cup boiling water
1 cup milk
4 eggs, separated
1 cup grated sharp cheddar cheese

1 can frozen condensed cream of shrimp soup
½ soup can white wine
½ pound cooked and cleaned small shrimp, fresh, frozen, or canned and drained

Scald the cornmeal by pouring the salted boiling water over it and stirring well until mixed. Add milk and egg yolks, mix thoroughly, and then add pepper and grated cheese. Beat the egg whites until stiff and fold into the cornmeal mixture gently. Turn into a hot buttered five-cup ring mold. Bake in a 350° oven about 35–40 minutes until puffy and lightly browned. Meanwhile, heat the frozen cream of shrimp soup with the ½ can of white wine (measuring by the soup can) and the shrimp. Unmold the ring of spoonbread onto a small warm plate or platter, and pour the shrimp sauce in the center. If desired, surround the ring with cold cherry tomatoes.

SERVE WITH

Fresh fruit

SHRIMP CURRY

In Charleston where the shrimp is very plentiful and very good, it is even eaten cold for breakfast with hot hominy and cold tomatoes. It needs almost no cooking time, at most 5–7 minutes and is, I think, best peeled before cooking—best for flavor and best for simplicity for the cook.

2 tablespoons butter
1 medium-sized onion, chopped fine
⅓ cup chopped green apple
⅓ cup chopped celery
2 tablespoons good curry powder, preferably the Madras brand

1 cup chicken broth or water
1½ pounds uncooked shrimp, peeled and cleaned
1 cup cream, either table or whipping (depending upon your figure and your pocketbook)
Salt and pepper

Cook the onion, apple, celery, and curry powder in the butter briefly. Add the broth or water and simmer until tender and the liquid has been reduced. Add the cream and uncooked shrimp. Simmer gently until cream is slightly reduced and shrimp a pale pink. Serves 4 to 6.

SERVE WITH

Yellow rice cooked in chicken broth
Chutney or Chinese plum sauce, chopped peanuts or almonds, grated coconut and crumbled cooked bacon

COQUILLES ST. JACQUES

The delicate meat of scallops needs delicate and brief cooking and delicate seasoning. One of the best ways is this classic dish which is usually served in individual baking shells that can be found in almost all houseware departments of good stores or ones specializing in classic cooking equipment.

1 pound sea or bay scallops	¼ pound sliced fresh mush-
¼ cup (½ stick) butter	rooms
1 shallot, finely chopped or 1	¼ teaspoon pepper—*no* salt
small white onion, chopped	¼ cup dry white wine
	Bread crumbs

Cut the scallops in quarters, if the large ones; in thirds for the small ones. Simmer in the butter with the shallot or onion and the mushrooms 2–3 minutes over medium heat. Add wine and cook only a minute or two more. Put in the scallop shells or a small casserole and sprinkle top with bread crumbs. Dot with butter and bake in 500° oven for 3 minutes. Serve immediately. Serves 4.

SERVE WITH

Rice cooked in chicken broth with white raisins and a lump of butter

Marinated cooked leeks and celery

Hot party rolls

SKEWERED SCALLOPS

The plain frozen scallops seem better in this recipe than the breaded ones, but either may be used, and, of course, if you can get the fresh ones so much the better. There is also a choice of whether you wish to use fresh mushrooms or water chestnuts, between the scallops, on the skewers. The mushrooms do indeed give a wonderful flavor and the water chestnuts a nice textural contrast.

2 packages frozen scallops, 7 ounces each (plain or breaded), or 1 pound fresh scallops (either bay or sea)

24 fresh mushrooms or water chestnuts (from a large can) or 2 packages frozen whole mushrooms
8 slices bacon

Thaw scallops slightly, and take 8 small bamboo skewers (the very inexpensive kind available in Oriental stores). Thread 3 scallops and 3 mushrooms or water chestnuts alternately, putting a bacon slice in between. The bacon may be wound over one scallop and mushroom or cut into small pieces. Broil about 5 minutes on each side or until the bacon is crisp. Arrange two skewers for each serving on hot rice. Pour curry sauce over each serving, sprinkling with slivered almonds. The Armenians and the Persians whom I know would push the food off the skewer onto the plate, but Americans like to look at the skewers.

Streamlined Curry Sauce

1 can undiluted cream of chicken soup

½ cup chablis or other white wine
1 tablespoon curry powder

Mix and heat slowly, stirring constantly until almost to a boil, and simmer for a few minutes. Serves 4.

SERVE WITH

Rice
Slivered toasted almonds

Cherry tomatoes
Watermelon pickle

TORTILLA PIE WITH CLAM FILLING

This may be made in a streamlined fashion, using the canned tortillas or making some from scratch, preferably in a blender, following a crêpe recipe, but using corn meal instead of flour. Fry in a 6- or 7-inch pan, one at a time or more on a flat griddle.

1 can tortillas
Bacon fat
3 tablespoons butter
3 tablespoons flour
¼ cup white wine
1 tablespoon chopped chives
or parsley

½ teaspoon dried tarragon
3 cans minced clams (7-ounce size) or 2 cans baby whole Japanese clams (10-ounce size)

Spread the tortillas lightly with bacon fat and heat in oven, arranging on a cookie sheet. There are 18 tortillas to a can in one of the more widely distributed brands. Use 8–9 to one seafood pie. Make a sauce by melting the butter and adding the flour, stir and cook until thick and smooth. Add the juice from the clams a little at a time, stirring until smooth and thickened. Add the seasonings, the chives, parsley, and tarragon, stir until smooth and thick. Then add the wine a little at a time. Add the minced or baby Japanese clams (as tiny as an oyster crab) and cook until barely heated. Spread a spoonful at a time on the tortillas, building up in layers of not more than 8 or 9, using two stacks if necessary. Either serve immediately or keep warm until needed. To serve, cut in wedges. Serves 4 to 6.

SERVE WITH

Spinach salad (p. 158)
French bread

CRÊPES FOURNÉE

Crêpes Fournée is a delicately intricate dish of tender, thin pancakes, wrapped around a winey concoction of crabmeat baked in Mornay sauce.

Crabmeat Mixture

1 pound fresh crabmeat
1 teaspoon shallot, finely
   chopped
½ cup heavy cream

6 tablespoons butter
1 6-ounce glass white wine
1 teaspoon Dijon mustard
   Salt and pepper

Melt the butter; add the finely chopped shallot and the white wine. Cook slowly until reduced to about half the quantity. Add the heavy cream, mustard, salt and pepper to the crabmeat which has been carefully picked apart to remove the thin membranes. Cook over a low flame for 10 minutes.

Thin pancakes

¾ cup cake flour, sifted
1 tablespoon powdered sugar
2 tablespoons melted butter
2 eggs plus 2 egg yolks

1¾ cups milk
1 teaspoon cognac or rum
   Salt

Sift flour, powdered sugar and a pinch of salt. Beat eggs and mix with dry ingredients. Add milk slowly and stir until smooth. Last, add melted butter and liquor. Strain through a fine sieve. Make the batter at least 2 hours before using. To bake the cakes, put a little batter in a very hot skillet. Pour in a thin layer of batter, cook until brown on one side, turn over and brown on the other side. Cook quickly— long cooking toughens them.

2 cups béchamel (2 table-
spoons butter, 3 tablespoons
flour, 2 cups milk, and ¼
teaspoon salt)

¼ cup coarsely grated Swiss
cheese
Nutmeg
Salt and pepper

Melt butter in saucepan over low heat, blend in the flour, and cook slowly, stirring, until ingredients froth together for 2 minutes without coloring. Remove from heat and, as soon as *roux* has stopped bubbling, pour in the milk and salt, which have been heated to a boil. Immediately beat vigorously with a wire whip to blend, gathering all bits of *roux* from the inside edges of the pan. Set saucepan over moderately high heat and stir with the wire whip until béchamel comes to a boil. Boil for 1 minute, stirring. Then remove from heat and beat in the cheese until it has melted and blended with the sauce. Season to taste with salt, pepper, and a pinch of nutmeg. Put some of crabmeat mixture on each pancake, roll up, and place side by side in a buttered baking dish. Cover with Mornay Sauce and brown in a medium oven 10 minutes or until brown and bubbly.

SERVE WITH

Fresh or frozen asparagus, dressed with butter and lemon juice
French bread

This soup is one of the few served cold that is a meal in itself. It is a wonderfully soothing and simple dish that will smooth away your cares on a hot, hot night.

1 quart buttermilk or 1 pint sour cream, thinned with 1 cup bouillon and 1 cup white wine or 1 pint yogurt plus 2 cups wine
2 cups diced cucumbers
½ cup chopped green onions, tops and bottoms
¾ cup diced, cooked cold beef, chicken, or flaked fish
1 cup cooked shrimp or crab or lobster
¼ cup fresh chopped dill or 1 teaspoon of crushed dill seed or ½ finely chopped dill pickle
¼ cup chopped parsley
2 hard-cooked eggs, sliced
Salt and pepper

Chill all together for two to three hours or more, except the egg. Serve very cold in large shallow soup bowls with an ice cube in each dish. Float several slices of egg in each bowl. Sprinkle with more parsley. When serving, make sure that each bowl has some of everything. Serves 4.

SERVE WITH

Hot piroshki—basically these are filled rolls or biscuits—a reasonable variant may be made with the refrigerated tube biscuits and some chopped sautéed onion or Smithfield ham-spread or sautéed mushrooms, spread on each biscuit before pinching together and baking

ACORN SQUASH STUFFED WITH CREAMED OYSTERS

Acorn squash halves are tidy and decorative edible and individual casseroles. For generous servings, allow two acorn halves for each serving.

4 acorn squash, cut in half
4 tablespoons butter
1 can undiluted cream of celery soup
1 pint fresh oysters or 1 package frozen

2 slices crumbled, crisp cooked bacon
1 tablespoon finely chopped

Simmer the oysters in their juice until the edges ruffle. Mix with the celery soup and divide into the acorn halves. The acorn halves should be baked before filling for ½ hour in a 350° oven with a half-pat of butter in each one. The unfilled acorn halves may be pre-baked and then filled and baked again just before serving. Sprinkle the tops with the crumbled, cooked bacon and the parsley. Bake for 15 minutes. Serves 4.

SERVE WITH

Broiled tomato halves topped with sour cream and finely chopped dill, or cucumber or onion spread with this mixture before broiling
Hard rolls

CRAB PILAF

This is best made with the fresh lump crabmeat but the frozen King crab from the Pacific Coast will do, as will the canned.

1 pound crabmeat, preferably the lump or backfin
4 strips of bacon
2 medium-sized onions, finely chopped
1 clove garlic, chopped fine
1 cup raw rice
2 cups white wine
¼ cup cognac
¼ cup chopped parsley
2 tomatoes, peeled, seeded, and chopped
Salt
Freshly ground black pepper
½ cup heavy or sour cream

Sauté the bacon in a heavy cold skillet to start with, and heat slowly until crisp. Remove the bacon. Add onion, garlic, and rice to the bacon fat. Cook until onion is transparent and also the rice. Add wine, parsley, bring to a boil, cover, turn heat down low, and cook for 15–20 minutes or until liquid is absorbed. Stir in the cognac, chopped tomato, crabmeat, and bacon and cook just hot. Stir in the cream just before serving. Serves 4.

SERVE WITH

Green beans amandine
Biscuits

ROAST HAUNCH OF SALMON

Salmon is best eaten on its home grounds in cold places, such as Canada, Washington state, Scotland, etc. It is seldom seen elsewhere except in steaks or cans, although your fish man will have it whole. A big piece of meat cut from the center part is not only festive and delicious but what is not consumed at the time makes the very best salads and soufflés. Except for color, it does not much resemble that in cans, and is less expensive.

1 piece (4 to 5 pounds) of fresh salmon	1 stalk celery, chopped
1 pint white wine	1 lemon, sliced thin and seeds removed
1 onion, chopped	Salt and pepper

Arrange the haunch of salmon in a baking dish still in its shining silver skin. Add the rest of the ingredients except the salt and pepper, and roast in the oven at 350° for about an hour, basting from time to time with pan liquid. When done, the salmon should flake easily with a fork. Let cool in the liquid. I prefer to serve the salmon with its skin still on. It makes a very handsome dish, especially when served cold on a platter surrounded by finely chopped wine and chicken aspic. Serves lots. This is the time you *want* leftovers.

SERVE WITH

> Cucumbers, sliced, with French dressing
> Spoonbread (p. 191)

Cheese, Eggs, Pasta and Vegetables

FRIED CHEESE

In Holland, slices of Gouda or Edam cheese are fried and served as a luncheon dish with a salad and wine or beer. This is also a good accompaniment to hamburgers, the big thick type, nice and juicy.

2 egg whites, beaten with 2 tablespoons water, or 2 whole eggs, slightly beaten
8 slices Gouda or Edam cheese ¼ to ½ inch thick, rind removed

1 or more cups fine bread crumbs
3 tablespoons fat, preferably bacon (although butter may be used)

Dip the slices of cheese in the egg white, which is delicate, or the whole eggs, which are robust, and then in the crumbs until they are well covered. Fry the slices in the bacon fat, or, less traditionally, the butter, until golden on both sides and soft inside. Serves 4.

SERVE WITH

Hamburgers
Armenian raw salad—diced cucumbers, radishes, celery chopped walnuts, stuffed green olives or black pitted ripe olives, olive oil, vinegar, and salt

CHEESE TACOS WITH ITALIAN SAUCE

This is a melting pot dish with several ethnic strains amiably involved.

12 tortillas (a can holds 16)
  Canned green chiles

1 cup (8 ounces) whipped cream cheese

Crisp the tortillas a bit in the oven first. Mix the whipped cream cheese which has been softened at room temperature with 2 or 3 of the chiles, diced. The chiles vary slightly in size and people vary much in their individual tolerances. Put a tablespoon on each tortilla, roll up, and place them in a shallow, rectangular baking dish. The Mexican ones which are inexpensive and colorful have several sizes which are good for this dish. Chill the rolled up tortillas until the sauce is nearly ready.

Sauce

3 tablespoons fat, preferably bacon
2 medium-sized onions, sliced thin

¼ cup fresh mushrooms, sliced
3 cans tomato sauce
¼ cup sliced, pitted black olives

Sauté the onions in the fat and cook until pale yellow. Add the mushrooms and cook slowly until they are sort of wilted-looking. Add the tomato sauce and the black olives. Let simmer about 30 minutes until it is thick and unctuous looking. If it cooks down too fast, add ½ cup bouillon. Pour the sauce over them when ready. About 15 minutes before the sauce is finished, take the tortillas out of the refrigerator, and bake about 25 minutes until hot and bubbling. Serves 4.

SERVE WITH

Cucumbers in yogurt
Watermelon filled with mixed fruits

SPIEDINI ALLA ROMANO

Spiedini in Italian means skewered. This is their way of making a toasted cheese sandwich and, at the risk of being thought un-American, I think much preferable to ours, aesthetically and gastronomically.

1 long loaf French bread, cut in half lengthwise and then in 1½ inch chunks or 3 small French loaves, baked and cut the same way
1 pound mozzarella cheese

2 cloves garlic, minced
1½ cups olive oil
6 anchovy fillets, mashed, or 2 tablespoons anchovy paste

Skewer a hunk of bread, a hunk of cheese, a hunk of bread, and so on, until all skewers are filled. Either heat the garlic and olive oil together or let the garlic soak in the olive oil a while before using. Mix with the anchovy and brush the skewers of bread and cheese with the garlic, olive oil, and anchovy mixture on all sides. Broil until the bread is toasted and the cheese melted, turning occasionally. Serve immediately. Serves 4.

SERVE WITH

Cold cooked green beans amandine

WELSH RABBIT

Usually this is served on toast or crackers but I like to use toasted English muffins for a more substantial meal. Sometimes a slice of ham and a slice of tomato or a slice of tomato and a slice of fried eggplant can be put on the muffin and the cheese sauce poured over it, or the muffin can be spread with anchovy paste.

2 cups grated sharp cheese or 1 pound of wine cheddar cheese	1½ tablespoons prepared mustard
4 tablespoons butter	2 teaspoons Worcestershire sauce
1½ cups milk	Pepper and salt
4 eggs	

Put the butter in the top of a double boiler, add the cheese, mustard, Worcestershire sauce, salt and pepper. Stir until melted, then add the milk slowly. Remove the pan from the heat and beat in the eggs. Serves 4.

S E R V E   W I T H

> Lettuce, water cress, sliced avocado, grapefruit segments (fresh, frozen, or canned), white grapes, hearts of palm (expensive, not obligatory, but a nice, crisp surprise), French dressing

CHEESE TORTE

A smooth, simple yet not Spartan dish.

2 tablespoons butter	2 eggs
1 pint cottage cheese	Salt
2 tablespoons sour cream	1 9-inch unbaked pie shell

Mix the butter, cottage cheese, sour cream, eggs, and salt. Start in a cold oven set for 300°. Continue baking for 45 minutes. This is eaten hot with a cold salad. Serves 4.

S E R V E   W I T H

> Greek salad (p. 213)
> Pumpernickel bread

CHEESE SOUP, RANCH HOUSE STYLE

There are several cheese soups available now in the supermarkets that are all right to use as a sauce or when one is in a hurry, but much the best are still those made from scratch. It is a pleasurable dish to make with or without an electric blender.

4 hot dried red chili peppers or 2 teaspoons dried red peppers
1 clove garlic
½ medium-sized green pepper, seeds and stem removed
½ cup chopped celery
½ cup chopped onions
3 tablespoons chicken fat or butter

3 tablespoons flour
½ cup dry white wine or consommé
1 quart milk
1 pound grated cheddar cheese Chopped chives or ½ cup Italian green beans, cooked until barely tender

The seasonings, the hot chili peppers, garlic, green pepper, celery, and onions may be crumpled, minced, and chopped for an interesting texture or put in a blender and blended a few seconds. The flavor is good and it is simple, but you may miss the textural contrast. Melt the chicken fat or butter and add the flour and cook slowly until dry. Add the wine or consommé, slowly stirring until smooth and thickened. Add the chopped or blended vegetables and cook for 5–10 minutes before adding the milk a little at a time, stirring constantly until smooth. Add the cheese and stir until melted and smooth and blended. Serve in large warm soup bowls and sprinkle with chives or a few Italian green beans.

SERVE WITH

Sliced tomatoes sprinkled with basil
Onion rolls

CHILI CON QUESO WITH POLENTA

Chili Con Queso is a mixture of tomatoes, onions, green chiles, and cheese, cooked into a celestial mélange. It is usually used as a dip with fritos or tostadas, but it is equally good layered with polenta or corn meal mush, and baked. The authentic versions call for Monterey Jack cheese, which is not generally available in the East. Processed cheddar cheese, I must grudgingly admit, melts down to a smoother mixture than natural cheeses.

2 cups corn meal or polenta meal	1 can (#2½) plum tomatoes
2 teaspoons salt	2 cans peeled green chilies
5 cups boiling water	1 cup heavy cream
2 large onions, chopped	1 pound Monterey Jack cheese,
½ stick butter	diced or processed cheddar, cut in pieces

Stir the corn meal into salted boiling water in a large pot, adding the corn meal a handful at a time, and turning heat down after each addition so it will not splutter over you. Stir until smooth and thick. Turn into buttered mold and chill until firm. Meanwhile, sauté the onions in the butter and add the tomatoes and green chiles, which have been chopped, the cream, and the cheese. Cook until thickened. Cut the polenta in ½-inch slices and cover the bottom of the casserole. Add some of the Chili Con Queso, and repeat the layers until the ingredients are all used, ending up with the Chili on top. Bake 20–30 minutes in a 350° oven. Serves 4 to 6.

SERVE WITH

Diced cucumbers and radishes in sour cream
French or Armenian bread

MIMOSA EGGS

There are some benighted people who do not like eggs and for them I feel a great pity. This is a sophisticated presentation of stuffed eggs, unlike the picnic variety.

6 hard-cooked eggs	2 tablespoons mayonnaise
⅓ cup foie gras or liver paste or good, but less delicate, liverwurst	½ cup cold Béchamel sauce

Béchamel Sauce

1 tablespoon butter	½ cup chicken broth
1 tablespoon flour	

Melt the butter, add flour, and cook for 2–3 minutes to get rid of the floury taste. Add the chicken broth, a little at a time, stirring constantly until smooth and thickened. Cut the eggs in half lengthwise and place in a shallow serving dish. Remove the yolks. Fill the halves with foie gras. Mix the mayonnaise and the Béchamel sauce and pour over the eggs. Put the yolks through a sieve or a ricer and sprinkle on top. Serves 4. This usually is served cold, but may be heated.

SERVE WITH

Salade Niçoise (p. 206)
Club rolls

POACHED EGGS IN TOMATO RABBIT SAUCE

There are times when your spirits are too storm-tossed to cope with the varying textures and seasonings of everyday meals, and nothing seems to soothe so much as poached eggs, suitably embellished for a main meal. The best of these versions, of course, is Eggs Benedict with Hollandaise sauce, made with the very best butter. This is a simpler but good everyday version.

8 eggs, poached or steamed in what are called egg poachers
4 English muffins, split and toasted
2 cups tomato sauce (canned)
2 teaspoons Worcestershire sauce

½ teaspoon dry mustard
1½ cups grated, chopped cheddar cheese
Salt and pepper, if needed (the sauce has some)

Heat the tomato sauce in the top of a double boiler with the seasoning and the cheese. Let boil a minute or two, stirring until the cheese is melted. Place the toasted muffin halves on a warmed serving platter, or separate plate, and a poached egg on each half. Cover with the sauce. Serves 4.

SERVE WITH

Lima beans, cooked with butter
More toasted muffin halves, if wanted

SCALLOPED EGGS AND ONIONS

An old-fashioned, half-forgotten, and delectable combination.

8 eggs, hard-cooked and sliced
6 small white onions, sliced
6 slices crumbled, crisp cooked
  bacon
3 tablespoons butter
3 tablespoons flour

1½ cups milk and ½ cup cream
  or 2 cups half-and-half
Grated nutmeg
Salt and pepper
Coarse, fresh bread crumbs

Make a cream sauce by melting the butter and cooking with flour for a couple of minutes before adding the milk or cream, slowly. Stir constantly until smooth and thickened. Add a pinch (less than ¼ of a teaspoon) of nutmeg, salt, and pepper to suit your taste. Layer the onions and eggs and bacon in a fairly shallow casserole or baking dish, covering each layer with some of the cream sauce. Top with bread crumbs and, if wished, finely chopped chives. Bake 45–50 minutes at 350°. Serves 4.

SERVE WITH

> German sour bean salad—cooked limas, sliced raw onions, sour cream, vinegar, horse-radish, salt, pepper, and chopped parsley
> Toasted English muffins

SPANISH *SPANISH OMELET*

I am not stuttering, but what *we* think of as a Spanish omelet startles and dazes all Spaniards the first time they meet up with it. What *they* call a Spanish omelet is a potato and onion one, and is a little like the Italian frittata, more like the French omelette Parmentier.

⅓ cup olive oil
2 medium-sized potatoes,
  peeled and cubed

½ medium-sized onion,
  chopped
6 eggs, beaten
  Salt

Sauté the potatoes in the olive oil, moving them around in the pan until they are cooked but not browned. Remove and cook the onion until opaque but not brown. Remove from the skillet and drain off any surplus fat. There should be just a film on the bottom. It is better to let it cool first before reheating; otherwise it gets overheated. Mix the beaten eggs with the potatoes, onion, and salt, and pour into the hot skillet. Lift the edges slightly until the omelet is browned on the side, then turn on the other side and brown that too. Serves 4.

S E R V E   W I T H

    Ragout of tomatoes—diced, fresh, or canned tomatoes, chopped green pepper, onion, salt, paprika, a tiny bit of brown sugar, and cream, cooked together until thickened and well blended
French bread

SPECIAL SCRAMBLED EGGS

This dish was christened "messy eggs," I think admiringly, by a young cousin who delighted in eggs scrambled variously at various times, for a late, leisurely breakfast, an after-theater snack or just for sudden and unscheduled hungers. In other countries these variations have dignified names. In Denmark it's an *aeggekage,* in the south of France a *piperade,* and in Italy a *frittata,* and there are many others. There are no special rules except that the eggs be fresh, the added ingredients compatible and the cooking gentle and brief. In some of the good combinations, one of the ingredients is slightly acid and the other crisp, but not always. None should completely obliterate the delicate flavor of the eggs.

These are just a few of the combinations we have liked. Much depends upon the contents of the refrigerator and the pantry shelf.

Grated or diced cheese and
chopped canned green chilies

Crisp cooked bacon, minced
clams and juice

Thinly sliced zucchini cooked in
olive oil

Chopped fresh tomato, chopped
sweet bell pepper, and
chopped onion

Shrimp, raw mushrooms, and
sherry

Camembert cheese and white
wine

Tomato and bacon

Put the butter in a cold pan, add the ingredients, and heat slowly. Add the eggs, unbeaten, and stir with a wooden spoon until lightly cooked. Serve immediately.

SERVE WITH

Croissants or some other rich bread
Fresh fruit

ABSOLUTELY SUBLIME EGGS

These are eggs in their greatest hour and might even take the place of Eggs Benedict in my affection, if they were as available in many fine restaurants.

2 cups mushroom purée (p. 16)
4 softly poached eggs
2 tablespoons butter
2 tablespoons flour
⅓ clove garlic, finely chopped
½ cup milk or half-and-half

2 eggs, separated
3 tablespoons freshly grated Parmesan or ½ cup grated sharp cheddar cheese

Put ½ cup of the mushroom purée in the bottom of each of four individual china cocottes or individual au gratin dishes and place a poached egg on each. Melt the butter in a small saucepan and sauté garlic briefly. Add the flour and cook a minute or two, then add milk, slowly stirring all the while until smooth and thickened. Add grated cheese, stir, remove from the fire, and add egg yolks, blend well, and fold in stiffly beaten egg whites. Pile gently on each cocotte on top of the poached egg and mushroom mixture, spreading to the edges with a light and easy hand. Put in a 350° oven 25–30 minutes or until the top puffs up and springs back when lightly touched. Serves 4 in a surprisingly filling way.

SERVE WITH

Celery stalks cooked in chicken broth
Croissants

RIGATONI WITH ITALIAN SAUSAGE

Rigatoni is one of the largest of the many shapes of pasta, which many American often loosely call macaroni or spaghetti. It is a large, tubular one with ridges, is frequently stuffed, and should be so treated in this recipe. To stuff the easy way, use a pastry bag with a large opening. The Italians are apt to use a small spoon and their fingers. This recipe is not a classic version.

1 pound rigatoni	1 large can Italian plum to-
¾ cup cottage cheese	matoes
½ cup Muenster, finely chopped	1 small can tomato paste
¾ cup grated sharp cheddar	2 onions, sliced thin
1 pound ricotta	1 teaspoon oregano
1 pound mozzarella	4 tablespoons olive oil
2 cloves garlic, minced	½ pound sweet Italian sausage

Cook the rigatoni in a large pot of boiling, salted water until just barely tender—*al dente,* as the Italians say. Remove and drain. Mix the cottage cheese, finely chopped Muenster, and grated cheddar together (this is the unorthodox touch), and stuff the rigatoni with this mixture. While the rigatoni is boiling or even before, the tomato sauce should be started. The longer it cooks, the smoother and richer it becomes. Sauté the garlic and onion in the olive oil, transfer to an enameled ironware or plain enameled pot. Add tomatoes, and at this point the Italians sieve the seeds out, which is a bit tedious but makes a smoother, professional-looking sauce. Add tomato paste and 4 paste cans of water, the sausage removed from its skin, and oregano. Simmer over low heat, 2–3 hours if time permits. Add more water, a little at a time, as the mixture cooks down. Both the stuffed rigatoni and tomato sauce may be cooked ahead of time and the final dish prepared for later reheating. Put a layer of the stuffed rigatoni in a large shallow casserole or a lasagne baking dish, if you have one, add some of the ricotta and sliced mozzarella, and cover with tomato sauce. Repeat. Most lasagne dishes will hold two or three layers but you should end up with the tomato sauce and both ricotta and mozzarella on top. Bake 45 minutes to 1 hour in a 350° oven, or longer. This dish is rather adaptable to your time. Serves 4 to 6 generously.

Skordalia (p. 47)
Raw broccoli flowerets
Italian bread

SPAGHETTI AND ITALIAN MEAT SAUCE

One of the delights of Italian versions of meat sauce for spaghetti is that while no two Italians give you exactly the same recipe, all reek with a robust aroma and have a rich, lusty flavor.

2 tablespoons oil
1 clove garlic, crushed
1 teaspoon parsley, chopped
1 can medium-sized Italian plum tomatoes

2 cans Italian tomato paste
½ pound beef in one piece
1 pound fresh spareribs
½ pound Italian sausage

Heat oil, add garlic and parsley. Sauté for a few minutes. Add tomatoes, tomato paste, and 1 cup water. Simmer for 2 hours, stirring often. Brown beef, spareribs, and sausage, letting the sausage provide the fat. Add to the tomato sauce and simmer for another hour or until meat is cooked. This is enough sauce for 2 pounds of spaghetti and will generously serve 4 Italians, 8 others.

SERVE WITH

Spaghetti
Mixed green cooked vegetables—peas, green beans, limas
Italian bread

PASTA WITH ANCHOVY SAUCE

Pasta, in all its many fascinating shapes, varies a little in taste, not only with different sauces but in the different shapes. That is because there is a proportion of sauce to the pasta that makes a perceptible difference. So, you might try various shapes with this sauce, cooking a pound of the pasta in a large pot of boiling salted water until just barely tender, not mushy.

3 tablespoons butter
3 tablespoons olive oil
2 cloves garlic, minced

1 flat can anchovy fillets, or 4 generous tablespoons anchovy paste
⅓ cup finely chopped parsley

Heat the butter and olive oil together and then sauté the garlic in the olive oil, discarding the garlic later. Stir in the mashed anchovy fillets or the anchovy paste and blend well. Toss the hot, drained, cooked pasta in the sauce. The pasta should not be cooked until the last minute. Serves 4.

SERVE WITH

Broiled hamburgers (p. 40)
Tomatoes, stuffed with cream cheese and diced hard-cooked eggs (p. 36)
Italian bread

Spoonbread is more exactly a corn bread that is served with a table-spoon. It isn't eaten with a spoon but is served on a plate with lots of butter in place of mashed potatoes or rice and the bread you would serve with them. It is simple to make and there is no such thing as a poor one, though some are richer in eggs than others, and some are puffy like a soufflé. White corn meal, preferably water-ground with flecks of the yellow, is always used, according to the purists— which is to say, all southerners. On the other hand, the directions will work with the yellow corn meal prevalent in most regions.

1 cup white corn meal, prefer-ably water-ground	2 or 3 eggs, separated for the fluffy type
1 cup boiling water	2 tablespoons butter or, better yet, bacon drippings
1 teaspoon salt	
1 cup milk	

Scald corn meal by pouring the boiling water and salt over it in the mixing bowl. Stir in the milk, a little at a time, and the whole eggs if the plain spoonbread is desired. If the fluffy version is wanted, and many prefer it, stir in unbeaten egg yolks and then fold in the whites that have been stiffly beaten. Heat a shallow baking dish with the butter or drippings and turn the spoonbread into the heated fat. Bake in a 350° oven 45–50 minutes or until a golden brown. Serve onto the plate with lots more butter. Serves 4 to 6.

SERVE WITH

> Grilled chicken with chopped onion (p. 118)
> Pebre—a Chilean mishmash of chopped onion, diced tomatoes, hot green chili pepper, olive oil, vinegar, salt, and pepper

KASHA WITH SEA SHELLS

From the Baltic Sea to the Mediterranean, throughout central Europe and including Russia, cracked grains are cooked and eaten as a starch vegetable, supplanting sometimes potatoes, noodles, and rice. They are generally wheat or buckwheat, and usually have three different grinds and are called many, many different names in different countries. The most common are Kasha and Bulgur. Traditionally, the cereal is started in a cold skillet and stirred around with a raw egg but even the traditional housewife from the old country varies her own technique from time to time. This version of a Russian-born housewife cooking for a Polish-born husband is one which the American-born children adore. It is best, one of the daughters said, cooked with the juices from the roast beef much as the English do with their Yorkshire pudding.

1 cup kasha
1 small onion, finely chopped
2 tablespoons chicken fat or
   butter or cooking oil
3 cups beef bouillon

½ cup Italian sea shell pasta
   (the small size)
Salt and juices from roast
   beef (not obligatory but wonderful)

Sauté the kasha and the onion in the fat and stir with a spoon or fork until the onion is pale yellow. Add the broth, seasonings, and sea shells, bring to a boil and then reduce heat to low, cover, and simmer for about 20 minutes or until the liquid has been absorbed. Remove from heat and let stand 5–10 minutes before serving. If there is any meat juice, even from hamburgers, stir it in at this time. Serves 4.

SERVE WITH

Roast beef
Japanese persimmon salad—1 or 2 persimmons, a bit of
   chopped feathery fennel, water cress, and French dressing,
   gently tossed together

POTATOES BAKED WITH CARROTS

When time is limited and a recipe calls for cooked chicken, I prefer the ones cooked on an electric spit and available in many grocery stores to using canned chicken, which as my father used to say tastes too long dead. Naturally, if time permits it is less expensive to roast your own.

1 envelope instant potatoes (for 4 servings) mixed according to directions, using milk instead of water and 2 tablespoons of butter, or 2 cups mashed potatoes	1 cup water
	¼ cup melted butter
	1 teaspoon salt
	2 tablespoons sugar
	2 tablespoons cornstarch
1 pound raw carrots, sliced thin (about 3½–4 cups)	2 tablespoons lemon juice
	2 eggs

This is best done in a blender. If you do not have a blender, cook the carrots until tender, drain, and put through a food mill, or mash and mix with the rest of the ingredients. Otherwise, put ½ cup water in the blender, half of the melted butter, half the salt and sugar, and half the cornstarch and lemon juice. Put in a cupful of carrots at a time, blend, add a second cup, blend, and remove from blender. Blend the other half of the ingredients the same way. Mix with the mashed potatoes. Add unbeaten eggs (omit for low cholesterol diets), turn into a buttered casserole, and bake 35–40 minutes at 350°, or until lightly browned. Serves 4.

SERVE WITH

Roast or rotisserie chicken

Spring salad—dandelion leaves dressed with bacon and bacon drippings, vinegar, sugar, pepper, and onion, garnished with hard-cooked eggs

French bread

KUGELE

One shouldn't make sweeping statements, especially in print, but I think this is one of my favorite ways of cooking and eating potatoes. It is indeed best made from scratch, grating raw white potatoes. Unfortunately, this is not only an extremely tedious job even for Polish housekeepers used to it, but hazardous for those unskilled with a grater.

6 large potatoes, peeled and grated, or 2 packages potato pancake mix, prepared according to directions
3 or 4 strips bacon, cooked until crisp and then broken into pieces

¼ cup bacon fat
2 eggs
Salt and pepper
1 pint sour cream

Mix the potatoes with the bacon, bacon fat, seasonings and eggs, and turn into a shallow rectangular baking dish. Bake in a 350° oven 40–50 minutes. The top should be brown and crusty. Serve hot with a pitcher of cold sour cream. Serves 4 to 6.

SERVE WITH

Fresh cold, cooked asparagus with Gorgonzola sauce (crumbled Gorgonzola, vinegar, red wine, salt, and pepper)

CREAMED POTATOES

In the current vogue for serving rice with everything, brought on probably by the increasing interest in the different ethnic ways of cooking, some of the delightful ways of cooking potatoes are being overlooked and even lost to new generations.

¼ cup butter
¼ cup finely chopped celery
1 tablespoon flour
1 cup heavy cream

1 teaspoon salt
4 medium-sized potatoes, boiled and sliced

Sauté the celery in the butter and sprinkle with flour. Add the heavy cream and salt a little at a time. Cook until mixture becomes a thin sauce, stirring constantly. Arrange the sliced potatoes in a shallow baking dish and pour cream sauce over all. Bake briefly. Serves 4.

SERVE WITH

Roast baby turkey (p. 142)
Peas
Hot biscuits

BAKED POTATOES WITH FISH ROES

Baked potatoes which are so good in themselves, with plenty of butter and salt and pepper, take well to any kind (almost) of embellishment. The best fish roe in many people's minds is shad, which is expensive, whether seasonal and fresh or canned. But there are some inexpensive canned fish roes from anonymous fish which taste very well.

2 large baked Idaho potatoes, baked in their well-scrubbed and greased skins
2 fish roes or 1 can shad roe with 2 roes in it or 1 can fish roe

2 tablespoons lemon juice
4 tablespoons butter
Salt and pepper
½ teaspoon dried dill or 1 tablespoon finely chopped fresh dill

Break the baked potatoes in half with a fork, and fluff slightly. Cook the roes about a minute and a half in butter and lemon juice. Add the seasoning and divide into 4 parts, putting 1 part on each potato half. Bake briefly in a hot oven 2–3 minutes. Serves 4.

SERVE WITH

Sliced ham or meat loaf
Cooked frozen mixed vegetables marinated in French dressing and then drained and tossed in mayonnaise and sprinkled with capers
Butterflake rolls

SCALLOPED POTATOES PROVENÇAL

No wishy-washy dish, this.

4 medium-sized onions, sliced thin
2 tablespoons olive oil
5 fresh tomatoes, peeled and seeded and cut in squares
Salt
6 anchovies and 2 tablespoons of oil from the can or 1½ tablespoons anchovy paste and 2 more tablespoons olive oil

2 cloves garlic, chopped fine
6 medium-sized boiling potatoes, peeled and sliced thin
⅓ cup of grated cheese (Swiss or very sharp cheddar)
⅓ cup sliced black pitted olives

Sauté the onions in the olive oil over low heat until the onions are opaque but not colored. Add the tomato squares to the onions and salt. Mix the anchovies or anchovy paste with the garlic and the oil. Spread a third of the tomato and onion mixture on the bottom of a baking dish, then arrange one half the potato slices tidily in neat overlapping circles. Add the anchovy-oil mixture, some more tomato and onion, more potatoes, more anchovies, and top with the rest of the tomato and onions. Sprinkle top with the cheese and olives, and sprinkle with about a tablespoon more of olive oil over all. Bake in 400° oven for 40 minutes or until potatoes are tender. They should need no other juices except that from the tomatoes. However, tomatoes and potatoes vary in their moisture content so if they start to brown too fast, add ½ cup bouillon and cover with aluminum foil. Serves 4 to 6.

SERVE WITH

Swordfish steak (cooked like the Steak au Poivre on p. 15)

RED SWEET PEPPERS STUFFED WITH EGGPLANT

We are careless about our plenty and do not make the most of our abundant food. The Italians, who mostly have had to make do with less, care more about what they eat and make much of the foods they have. When they stuff peppers, they often use the spectacularly large and splendidly red ones.

4 sweet peppers, preferably red and very, very large (4–5 inches square)
1 medium-sized eggplant, peeled and diced
olive oil
1 small onion, finely chopped
1 clove garlic
2 plum tomatoes (canned)
¼ cup catsup

1 teaspoon oregano
⅓ cup freshly grated Parmesan cheese
1 tablespoon finely chopped parsley, Italian if possible
1 tablespoon finely chopped fresh basil or 1½ teaspoon dried basil
Salt and pepper

Cut the tops off the peppers and save to use as a lid. Carefully scrape out the seeds and white membrane, and put in ice water until needed. Cook the eggplant in the olive oil with the onion and the garlic. Add tomatoes or catsup, cheese and seasonings, and cook together for a few minutes. Remove garlic and mash in an electric blender. Fill the drained peppers and cover with the lids. Bake in a 350° oven 25–40 minutes until barely cooked. The peppers should be still firm and unwrinkled. Serve at room temperature. Serves 4. This is often used as a rather substantial antipasto.

SERVE WITH

Leg of lamb, cooked European style (p. 67)
Risi Pisi (p. 91)
Italian bread

SPINACH PANCAKES

In this country we are just beginning to discover and enjoy the exciting diversity of pancakes as they are served in some form or other at all parts of all meals in almost all countries and called many, many names. This one is basically a French crêpe with spinach added. It is a blissfully simple dish when the batter is made in an electric blender and not really very difficult made in an unautomated fashion. Like all pancake batters, it is better if it stands for several hours before using.

1 cup chopped spinach, fresh or
  frozen
1 cup milk
4 eggs

Salt
2 cups all-purpose flour, sifted
  before measuring
¼ cup melted butter

Pour boiling water over the spinach to blanch, and drain immediately, Put in the blender with the milk, eggs, 1 cup water, the flour, and the melted butter. Cover and blend for a minute or two. Turn blender off, scrape flour if it has adhered to the side, and blend a few seconds more. Chill covered in the refrigerator for at least 2 hours. If the crêpes are to be made in the unautomated way, purée the spinach in a food mill (or use the thawed creamed, frozen spinach). Beat the eggs, add milk, beat some more, add water, beat some more, then add flour a little at a time. Add the spinach and blend. The butter goes in last. You may use a rotary beater or a wire whip or, of course, an electric beater. The batter should be the consistency of coffee cream, just thick enough to coat a wooden spoon with a thin film. Because flour varies according to the moisture in the air, if the mixture seems too thick add a little more water a tablespoon at a time. Try one crêpe first to see. Use a small iron skillet or a crêpe pan about 6½–7 inches in diameter. Oil the pan by rubbing it with a piece of fat bacon or salt pork, or brush lightly with oil; using moderately high heat, let the skillet pre-heat enough to begin to smoke. Remove from the heat and pour ¼ cup of batter into the middle of the pan. Tilt in all directions so that the whole middle is covered. This should be done quickly. If there is any surplus, pour it back into the bowl. Cook about a minute and one half. At this point the dextrous exhibitionist can flip the crêpe; the more timid will lift it with a spatula. When it is browned slightly, turn over, rolling it lightly on the spatula, and cook very briefly on the other side, 20–30 seconds. Slide it onto a warm plate, grease the skillet, and repeat the rest of the procedure. Keep the crêpes warm in a very low oven, or make them ahead of time and reheat when needed. To serve, fold in quarters and allow three apiece. This should make about 12 six-inch crêpes. Serves 4.

SERVE WITH

Roast chicken
Water cress and raw mushrooms with French dressing
Hot biscuits

SPINACH, CHINESE STYLE

One of the basic principles of Chinese cooking is the brief cooking and artful seasoning.

1 pound fresh or 10-ounce package pre-washed spinach (frozen will not do for this)
1 clove garlic, minced
1 teaspoon salt

½ teaspoon sugar
¼ teaspoon monosodium glutamate
2 tablespoons peanut or corn oil

Wash the spinach and pat dry, and tear into pieces if bought loose. Over high heat, heat oil and crushed garlic in a skillet. Add the spinach and stir until the oil and spinach are well mixed. Fish out the garlic and add the salt, sugar, and monosodium glutamate. Stir for 2 minutes more and serve. Serves 4.

SERVE WITH

Roast leg of lamb (p. 65)
Noodles Romano—noodles with cheese dressing, packaged
Tossed salad with 4 or 5 kinds of greens, French dressing

This dish, which turns up in different spellings in Central European and Balkan cuisines, presents assembled vegetables with splendor. It is handsomest when baked in a shallow 16-inch enameled casserole or in a paella pan. Because at one time people did not often have huge ovens at home and so took their ghiveches to the village bakers to be cooked, traditionally they are served warm, but not hot. Their flavors do seem at their best when they are allowed to cool slightly when removed from the oven. While many vegetables are used, there is not a lot of each one. In this version some shortcuts in shopping and preparing the vegetables are used without impairing the essential character of the dish.

1 family-sized package of mixed frozen vegetables
1 package frozen broccoli
2 large onions, sliced thin
1 package frozen okra
1 small eggplant, cut in large cubes with peel left on
1 package frozen squash or ½ pound fresh sliced yellow squash

3 tomatoes, seeds removed, quartered
3 potatoes, peeled and diced
½ cup hot olive oil
1½ cup beef bouillon or chicken broth
1 bunch green seedless grapes, pulled from the stems
½ bunch chopped parsley
Salt and pepper

Parboil the potatoes for 10 minutes and drain. Blanch the eggplant in boiling salted water and drain. Arrange all the vegetables in the large shallow casserole. A deeper one will cook the vegetables adequately, of course, but does not present them so picturesquely. Arrange the vegetables in a design if you wish. Heat the oil and the broth together until boiling. Pour over all the vegetables and sprinkle the top with the chopped parsley and green grapes. Put in 350° oven and bake about 1¼ hour, until vegetables are fork-tender. A smaller amount would take less time. Serves 4 to 6.

SERVE WITH

Meat, if desired—roast lamb, lamb chops, pork chops, etc. French bread

CURRIED VEGETABLES

Most people think that most Indian food is curried, which is not true. It is true that the Indians add some of the seasonings that go to make up curry powder and often curry powder itself to some things we would not think of currying, such as vegetables.

1 tablespoon oil	2 medium-sized diced boiled
1 teaspoon ground cumin	potatoes
1 teaspoon dark brown mustard seed	½ small head boiled cauliflower (broken into flowerets)
1 tablespoon curry powder (the Indians I know use the Madras brand)	1 large or 2 small green peppers, sliced into rings
⅔ teaspoon ground coriander	2 raw medium-sized tomatoes, cut into chunks, seeds and
⅓ teaspoon red pepper	juice removed
	Salt

Heat the oil, add the seasonings, and stir. Add the cooked vegetables. Cook slowly in the curry mixture until lightly browned and wonderfully odorous. Serve with yogurt and fresh limes, cut in quarters. Serves 4.

SERVE WITH

Baked chicken with black walnuts (p. 107)
Hot toasted corn cakes

CORN PUDDING

In these days of plenty and great variety, it is astonishing to find how gratified people are when you serve them a corn pudding. This one is a deviation from the usual, in that it uses the delicate white shoe peg corn and has a base of undiluted cream of celery soup.

1 pound can white shoe peg corn, drained
3 eggs, beaten slighty
1 can cream of celery soup, undiluted
1 small can chopped pimientos
½ cup freshly grated Parmesan cheese

1 tablespoon cheese
1 tablespoon sugar
1 cup half milk and half cream
Salt and pepper

Mix all the ingredients together and turn into a low buttered casserole. Bake 35 minutes or more in a 350° oven. Serves 4.

S E R V E   W I T H

      Roast baby turkey (p. 142)
      Fresh asparagus
      Hot party rolls

ONION AND APPLE CASSEROLE

This dish is a fine accompaniment to roast duck or roast pork, or could be topped in the last 15–20 minutes of its baking by some sausage patties which have been fried first to get rid of some of the excess fat.

3 large onions, sliced thin
4 large or 6 smaller apples, sliced, peeled, and cored

Chicken broth or beef bouillon enough to almost cover (about 2 cups or more)
Salt and pepper
Bread crumbs, plain or seasoned

The amount of liquid, bread crumbs, and butter will vary somewhat with the size of your casserole and the size onions or apples you use. Put a layer of onion, a layer of apples, seasoning, and bread crumbs, and dot with butter. Repeat until all the ingredients are used. Bake for 1 hour in a 350° oven. Serves 4.

SERVE WITH

> Meat (see above)
> Yorkshire pudding (basic recipe or popover mix)

ST. GERMAIN TART

This tart has a thin filling with a robust, concentrated smoky flavor.

1 package smoky green pea
  soup
1 pint sour cream
2 tablespoons gin

1 baked 8-inch pie shell
½ cup fresh cooked peas

Mix the smoky green pea soup with the sour cream and gin and let stand for 2–3 hours or until the peas have softened and the flavors mingled. Turn mixture into the baked pie shell and sprinkle the fresh peas on top. Cook in slow oven (350°) for 20 minutes. Serves 4.

SERVE WITH

> Baked ham
> Water cress
> Hot biscuits

LEEK CUSTARD

Leeks are not properly understood in America or widely available, except in large cities. If they cannot be bought in your region, spring onions may be substituted but will not be quite the same.

8 leeks, trimmed, halved, and cut into 2-inch pieces and parboiled 15 minutes or 2 bunches spring onions, cut in 1½-inch pieces and parboiled 5 minutes

1 unbaked 9-inch pie shell
2 cups evaporated milk or half cream and half milk
4 eggs, beaten with 2 additional egg yolks

Scald the milk or half-and-half and pour over the beaten egg. Beat together briefly. Add salt and pepper. Drain the leeks or onions, and strew on the bottom of the pie shell. Pour in the custard mixture. Bake 55 minutes at 325° or until a knife inserted comes out clean. Serve warm, but not hot. Serves 4.

SERVE WITH

Fried chicken (p. 110)
Cherry tomatoes
Hot biscuits

SMOKY PEA SOUFFLÉ

The dehydrated smoky pea soup is fine as a soup, as a cocktail dip when mixed with sour cream, or as this vegetable dish.

1 package dehydrated Swiss smoky green pea soup
1 cup sour cream

4 eggs, separated
(No extra seasoning, the soup has enough)

Mix the dehydrated soup with the sour cream and let stand in the refrigerator at least 2 hours, until the peas soften. Stir in the egg yolks,

whip the whites until stiff, and fold in gently. Tu.
greased soufflé dish with straight sides. Bake in 3
minutes, or until the top springs back when lightly
immediately. Serves 4.

SERVE WITH

> Lamb kidney chops, with a teaspoon of butter and tarragon
> on each
> Romaine, slivered cooked green beans, sliced beets, French
> dressing
> Pepper rolls

GREEN TOMATO PIE

You cannot make a green tomato pie just anywhere, any day, but when
the tomatoes are available they give this menu unusual diversity.

4 cups unpeeled green tomatoes cut in thin wedges	¼ teaspoon allspice
½ cup sugar	1 tablespoon lemon juice
2 tablespoons flour	3 tablespoons butter
Grated rind of 1 lemon	1 unbaked 9-inch pie shell or a pastry top

This may be made in a regular pie shell or in a baking dish with just
a pastry top. Either way, mix the sugar, flour, lemon rind, seasonings,
and butter together. Put a layer of tomato wedges in the casserole or
pie shell and sprinkle with the spicy mixture. Repeat, if you are using
a deep baking dish. If just using the pastry top, bake ¾ of an hour
in a 350° oven. If using pie shell and pastry top, bake one hour.
Serves 4.

SERVE WITH

> Barbecued lamb shanks (p. 62)
> Sliced lemon and orange and water cress salad, dressed with
> olive oil and finely chopped mint
> French or Armenian bread

This is a mixed vegetable salad as served in the south of France. You will never get the same directions from any two people, though there are certain invariables, such as fresh tomato, black olives, and anchovies.

3 tomatoes, peeled, quartered and seeded

½ cup tiny wrinkled black olives, drained (the kind bought in Greek stores from wooden tubs)

3 cooked new potatoes, sliced

⅓ tin fillets of anchovies, cut in pieces

3 hard-cooked eggs, quartered

Few slices raw green pepper

1 tablespoon capers

Dressing (4 parts olive oil, one part vinegar, salt, pepper, and ½ teaspoon Dijon mustard)

This salad may be tossed or, somewhat untraditionally, may be arranged decoratively in a design to please the eye, and sprinkled with the dressing. Serves 4 to 6.

SERVE WITH

"21" hamburgers (p. 40)
French bread

AVOCADO MOUSSE

It is, I believe, impossible to improve upon avocado eaten from the shell with just a little salt or even without it, but this dish is delicate and dramatic and will impress your family or guests.

2 envelopes plain gelatin	1½ cups puréed avocado
⅓ cup lemon juice	(1 large or 2 small)
¼ teaspoon salt	½ cup sour cream

Soften gelatin in ½ cup cold water. Add one cup boiling water and stir until dissolved. Add lemon juice and salt, and stir until the thickness of unbeaten egg whites. Mix the avocado purée and stir until thoroughly blended. Add sour cream. Turn into a 3-cup ring mold rinsed first in cold water, and chill until firm. Serves 6 to 8.

SERVE WITH

> Sliced turkey, ham, and tongue in aspic (p. 94) or any cold meat
>
> Water cress, for a crisp textural and color contrast—fill center with grapefruit and orange sections

LETTUCE STUFFED WITH ALMONDS

As we have said, everything in which mixtures of rice is stuffed or wrapped make the same mixture of rice taste a little different. The lettuce is somewhat unusual as a dolma.

12 large lettuce leaves	Salt
½ cup rice	3 tablespoons unsalted butter,
½ cup slivered almonds	softened at room temperature
1 teaspoon grated orange rind	1 cup orange juice

Mix the rice with the almonds, orange rind, and soft butter. Place a tablespoon or so on each leaf and roll up, folding in the ends. Arrange lettuce rolls on the bottom of a ceramic or enameled pie dish. Pour in the orange juice, and bake 30–40 minutes in a 350° oven, basting from time to time. Serves 4.

SERVE WITH

Roast leg of lamb (p. 65)
Baked eggplant and cheese (p. 64)
Pideh

BARLEY PILAF

Barley pilaf is *in* again after many decades of unwarranted obscurity. It is as easy as rice to prepare, requiring no peeling, and it doesn't sprout when stored. It is a delectable addition to meals otherwise too routine.

4 tablespoons butter	1 cup barley
1 medium-sized onion, chopped	2 cups consommé
¼ pound sliced fresh mush-rooms	½ teaspoon salt

Cook the onion, mushrooms, and barley in butter in a heavy skillet over medium heat, stirring frequently with a wooden spoon until the barley has a toasted light brown color and a nutty flavor. Turn the barley into a casserole, add the consommé which has been brought to a boiling point, cover and bake 50–60 minutes in a 350° oven. Serves 4.

S E R V E   W I T H

Broiled lamb chops
Water cress and lettuce with French dressing
Sesame seed rolls

RICE PILAF

This is rice cooked in the Indian fashion, according to the directions of Mrs. Jugran, whose husband is with the Indian Embassy in Washington.

2 tablespoons fat
1 medium onion, chopped
1 teaspoon ground cloves
1 teaspoon cumin
1 cup rice, soaked 1 hour in hot water

1 teaspoon salt
2 cups boiling water
¼ cup seedless raisins
⅓ cup blanched whole almonds

Cook the onions in the fat, add the cloves and cumin, and stir until the onions are pale yellow but not brown. Add the soaked and drained rice, the salt, boiling water, and raisins. Bring to a boil, cover, turn heat down low, and cook for about 20–25 minutes without looking. Remove the lid and fluff with a fork, and let stand a moment for any excess moisture to dry out. Add the almonds. Serves 4.

SERVE WITH

Sliced cooked ham in parsley (p. 88)
Hot sesame seed rolls

FRIED RICE

It is sometimes difficult to know what is the difference between a risotto, a fried rice, or a pilaf, and actually all are more or less the same. The rice is cooked in fat and then bits of this and bits of that, indigenous to the country, added, and who is to say what country it is, when here we have most of the ingredients available. This version is more or less Japanese.

½ stick butter
1 large onion, chopped
1½ cups brown rice
⅓ cup fresh chopped parsley
⅓ cup finely chopped celery

1 cup diced, cooked meat (pork, beef, or tongue)
1 pound can kidney beans, drained
4 cups beef bouillon

Sauté the onion in the butter and then the rice. Add the parsley, celery, and bouillon. Bring to a boil, cover, turn heat down low, and cook 20–30 minutes, or until rice has absorbed the liquid. Remove the lid and fluff rice with a fork, add the kidney beans, and serve. (Brown rice takes more liquid than white rice and longer cooking time.) Serves 4 to 6.

SERVE WITH

Tossed green salad
Ambrosia

FRIED CREAM

This odd-sounding and ambrosial dish is served as a desert in San Francisco and with fried chicken on our southeastern coast. Basically, it is a custard baked about ⅓ of an inch deep, chilled and cut in squares, rolled in crumbs and sautéed until brown. The thickenings vary from coast to coast, the southeastern inclination being to thicken with cornstarch while some chefs on the west coast use farina. This is a southeastern version.

1 stick cinnamon	½ tablespoon vanilla
1 pint milk	2 eggs, slightly beaten with water
⅓ cup sugar	
2 tablespoons cornstarch	Ground nuts, almonds, walnuts, or (for those who enjoy their gamey flavor) black walnuts
1 tablespoon flour	
3 tablespoons more milk (for mixing with the thickening)	
3 egg yolks, beaten	Sifted cracker crumbs
1 tablespoon butter	

Simmer the cinnamon and milk. Just before it comes to a boil, add the sugar, cornstarch, and flour which have been mixed with the other milk. Stir over low heat for 2–3 minutes. Remove from fire, add a spoon of the hot mixture to the beaten yolks, mix, and add to the rest of the hot milk. Heat over low fire and stir with a wooden spoon until barely cooked. Remove the cinnamon stick and discard, add butter and vanilla, and stir. Pour into a deep buttered pyrex rectangular platter or baking dish that is large enough so that the mixture is ⅓– ½ inch deep. Chill until quite firm, cut into finger-shaped strips 1″ x 2″ x 3″. Roll in cracker crumbs until thoroughly covered, then into the egg beaten with water, and then into more crumbs or ground nuts. Sauté in more butter over low heat until lightly browned on both sides. Put in a hot oven 4–5 minutes to soften. Serves 4 to 6.

SERVE WITH

Fried chicken (p. 110)
Fresh asparagus

GREEK SALAD

This is a Florida version; there are lots of Greeks in Florida, diving for sponges. There are no hard and fast rules except that it must be very aromatic and robustly flavored with such things as salty Greek feta cheese and anchovies and whatever fresh and vigorous odds and ends of vegetables you would like to add.

6 anchovies	1 medium-sized cucumber, peeled and diced
½ head lettuce, shredded	
1 heart celery, tops and bottoms, chopped	⅔ cup Greek chives, the small wrinkled kind bought in Greek and Italian groceries
1 sweet red onion, sliced paper thin	¼ pound feta cheese, crumbled
1 sweet bell pepper, red or green, cut in pieces with seed and membrane removed	⅓ cup olive oil
	2 tablespoons fresh lemon juice or 1 tablespoon vinegar
	Salt, pepper, and oregano

Mix the lettuce, celery, cucumber, tomatoes, onion, and pepper loosely in a bowl or arrange on a platter. Sprinkle the cheese on top and arrange the anchovies in a symmetrical fashion. Drizzle the oil over the salad and then the lemon juice and vinegar and the seasoning. Serves 4 to 6, amply.

SERVE WITH

Roast leg of lamb (p. 65)
Pideh—Armenian bread

INDEX

215

A CATALOGUE OF SELECTED DOVER BOOKS
IN ALL FIELDS OF INTEREST

A CATALOGUE OF SELECTED DOVER BOOKS
IN ALL FIELDS OF INTEREST

LEATHER TOOLING AND CARVING, Chris H. Groneman. One of few books concentrating on tooling and carving, with complete instructions and grid designs for 39 projects ranging from bookmarks to bags. 148 illustrations. 111pp. 7⅞ x 10.
23061-9 Pa. $2.50

THE CODEX NUTTALL, A PICTURE MANUSCRIPT FROM ANCIENT MEXICO, as first edited by Zelia Nuttall. Only inexpensive edition, in full color, of a pre-Columbian Mexican (Mixtec) book. 88 color plates show kings, gods, heroes, temples, sacrifices. New explanatory, historical introduction by Arthur G. Miller. 96pp. 11⅜ x 8½.
23168-2 Pa. $7.50

AMERICAN PRIMITIVE PAINTING, Jean Lipman. Classic collection of an enduring American tradition. 109 plates, 8 in full color—portraits, landscapes, Biblical and historical scenes, etc., showing family groups, farm life, and so on. 80pp. of lucid text. 8⅜ x 11¼.
22815-0 Pa. $4.00

WILL BRADLEY: HIS GRAPHIC ART, edited by Clarence P. Hornung. Striking collection of work by foremost practitioner of Art Nouveau in America: posters, cover designs, sample pages, advertisements, other illustrations. 97 plates, including 8 in full color and 19 in two colors. 97pp. 9⅜ x 12¼.
20701-3 Pa. $4.00
22120-2 Clothbd. $10.00

THE UNDERGROUND SKETCHBOOK OF JAN FAUST, Jan Faust. 101 bitter, horrifying, black-humorous, penetrating sketches on sex, war, greed, various liberations, etc. Sometimes sexual, but not pornographic. Not for prudish. 101pp. 6½ x 9¼.
22740-5 Pa. $1.50

THE GIBSON GIRL AND HER AMERICA, Charles Dana Gibson. 155 finest drawings of effervescent world of 1900-1910: the Gibson Girl and her loves, amusements, adventures, Mr. Pipp, etc. Selected by E. Gillon; introduction by Henry Pitz. 144pp. 8¼ x 11⅜.
21986-0 Pa. $3.50

STAINED GLASS CRAFT, J.A.F. Divine, G. Blachford. One of the very few books that tell the beginner exactly what he needs to know: planning cuts, making shapes, avoiding design weaknesses, fitting glass, etc. 93 illustrations. 115pp.
22812-6 Pa. $1.50

CREATIVE LITHOGRAPHY AND HOW TO DO IT, Grant Arnold. Lithography as art form: working directly on stone, transfer of drawings, lithotint, mezzotint, color printing; also metal plates. Detailed, thorough. 27 illustrations. 214pp.

21208-4 Pa. $3.00

DESIGN MOTIFS OF ANCIENT MEXICO, Jorge Enciso. Vigorous, powerful ceramic stamp impressions — Maya, Aztec, Toltec, Olmec. Serpents, gods, priests, dancers, etc. 153pp. 6⅛ x 9¼.

20084-1 Pa. $2.50

AMERICAN INDIAN DESIGN AND DECORATION, Leroy Appleton. Full text, plus more than 700 precise drawings of Inca, Maya, Aztec, Pueblo, Plains, NW Coast basketry, sculpture, painting, pottery, sand paintings, metal, etc. 4 plates in color. 279pp. 8⅜ x 11¼.

22704-9 Pa. $4.50

CHINESE LATTICE DESIGNS, Daniel S. Dye. Incredibly beautiful geometric designs: circles, voluted, simple dissections, etc. Inexhaustible source of ideas, motifs. 1239 illustrations. 469pp. 6⅛ x 9¼.

23096-1 Pa. $5.00

JAPANESE DESIGN MOTIFS, Matsuya Co. Mon, or heraldic designs. Over 4000 typical, beautiful designs: birds, animals, flowers, swords, fans, geometric; all beautifully stylized. 213pp. 11⅜ x 8¼.

22874-6 Pa. **$5.00**

PERSPECTIVE, Jan Vredeman de Vries. 73 perspective plates from 1604 edition; buildings, townscapes, stairways, fantastic scenes. Remarkable for beauty, surrealistic atmosphere; real eye-catchers. Introduction by Adolf Placzek. 74pp. 11⅜ x 8¼.

20186-4 Pa. $2.75

EARLY AMERICAN DESIGN MOTIFS. Suzanne E. Chapman. 497 motifs, designs, from painting on wood, ceramics, appliqué, glassware, samplers, metal work, etc. Florals, landscapes, birds and animals, geometrics, letters, etc. Inexhaustible. Enlarged edition. 138pp. 8⅜ x 11¼.

22985-8 Pa. $3.50
23084-8 Clothbd. $7.95

VICTORIAN STENCILS FOR DESIGN AND DECORATION, edited by E.V. Gillon, Jr. 113 wonderful ornate Victorian pieces from German sources; florals, geometrics; borders, corner pieces; bird motifs, etc. 64pp. 9⅜ x 12¼.

21995-X Pa. $2.75

ART NOUVEAU: AN ANTHOLOGY OF DESIGN AND ILLUSTRATION FROM THE STUDIO, edited by E.V. Gillon, Jr. Graphic arts: book jackets, posters, engravings, illustrations, decorations; Crane, Beardsley, Bradley and many others. Inexhaustible. 92pp. 8⅛ x 11.

22388-4 Pa. $2.50

ORIGINAL ART DECO DESIGNS, William Rowe. First-rate, highly imaginative modern Art Deco frames, borders, compositions, alphabets, florals, insectals, Wurlitzer-types, etc. Much finest modern Art Deco. 80 plates, 8 in color. 8⅜ x 11¼.

22567-4 Pa. $3.00

HANDBOOK OF DESIGNS AND DEVICES, Clarence P. Hornung. Over 1800 basic geometric designs based on circle, triangle, square, scroll, cross, etc. Largest such collection in existence. 261pp.

20125-2 Pa. $2.50

150 MASTERPIECES OF DRAWING, edited by Anthony Toney. 150 plates, early 15th century to end of 18th century; Rembrandt, Michelangelo, Dürer, Fragonard, Watteau, Wouwerman, many others. 150pp. 8⅜ x 11¼.   21032-4 Pa. $3.50

THE GOLDEN AGE OF THE POSTER, Hayward and Blanche Cirker. 70 extraordinary posters in full colors, from Maîtres de l'Affiche, Mucha, Lautrec, Bradley, Cheret, Beardsley, many others. 9⅜ x 12¼.   22753-7 Pa. $4.95
21718-3 Clothbd. $7.95

SIMPLICISSIMUS, selection, translations and text by Stanley Appelbaum. 180 satirical drawings, 16 in full color, from the famous German weekly magazine in the years 1896 to 1926. 24 artists included: Grosz, Kley, Pascin, Kubin, Kollwitz, plus Heine, Thöny, Bruno Paul, others. 172pp. 8½ x 12¼.   23098-8 Pa. $5.00
23099-6 Clothbd. $10.00

THE EARLY WORK OF AUBREY BEARDSLEY, Aubrey Beardsley. 157 plates, 2 in color: Manon Lescaut, Madame Bovary, Morte d'Arthur, Salome, other. Introduction by H. Marillier. 175pp. 8½ x 11.   21816-3 Pa. $3.50

THE LATER WORK OF AUBREY BEARDSLEY, Aubrey Beardsley. Exotic masterpieces of full maturity: Venus and Tannhäuser, Lysistrata, Rape of the Lock, Volpone, Savoy material, etc. 174 plates, 2 in color. 176pp. 8½ x 11.   21817-1 Pa. $4.00

DRAWINGS OF WILLIAM BLAKE, William Blake. 92 plates from Book of Job, Divine Comedy, Paradise Lost, visionary heads, mythological figures, Laocoön, etc. Selection, introduction, commentary by Sir Geoffrey Keynes. 178pp. 8½ x 11.
22303-5 Pa. $3.50

LONDON: A PILGRIMAGE, Gustave Doré, Blanchard Jerrold. Squalor, riches, misery, beauty of mid-Victorian metropolis; 55 wonderful plates, 125 other illustrations, full social, cultural text by Jerrold. 191pp. of text. 8⅛ x 11.
22306-X Pa. $5.00

THE COMPLETE WOODCUTS OF ALBRECHT DÜRER, edited by Dr. W. Kurth. 346 in all: Old Testament, St. Jerome, Passion, Life of Virgin, Apocalypse, many others. Introduction by Campbell Dodgson. 285pp. 8½ x 12¼.   21097-9 Pa. $6.00

THE DISASTERS OF WAR, Francisco Goya. 83 etchings record horrors of Napoleonic wars in Spain and war in general. Reprint of 1st edition, plus 3 additional plates. Introduction by Philip Hofer. 97pp. 9⅜ x 8¼.   21872-4 Pa. $3.00

ENGRAVINGS OF HOGARTH, William Hogarth. 101 of Hogarth's greatest works: Rake's Progress, Harlot's Progress, Illustrations for Hudibras, Midnight Modern Conversation, Before and After, Beer Street and Gin Lane, many more. Full commentary. 256pp. 11 x 14.   22479-1 Pa. $7.00
23023-6 Clothbd. $13.50

PRIMITIVE ART, Franz Boas. Great anthropologist on ceramics, textiles, wood, stone, metal, etc.; patterns, technology, symbols, styles. All areas, but fullest on Northwest Coast Indians. 350 illustrations. 378pp.   20025-6 Pa. $3.50

MOTHER GOOSE'S MELODIES. Facsimile of fabulously rare Munroe and Francis "copyright 1833" Boston edition. Familiar and unusual rhymes, wonderful old woodcut illustrations. Edited by E.F. Bleiler. 128pp. 4½ x 6⅜. 22577-1 Pa. $1.00

MOTHER GOOSE IN HIEROGLYPHICS. Favorite nursery rhymes presented in rebus form for children. Fascinating 1849 edition reproduced in toto, with key. Introduction by E.F. Bleiler. About 400 woodcuts. 64pp. 6⅞ x 5¼. 20745-5 Pa. $1.00

PETER PIPER'S PRACTICAL PRINCIPLES OF PLAIN & PERFECT PRONUNCIATION. Alliterative jingles and tongue-twisters. Reproduction in full of 1830 first American edition. 25 spirited woodcuts. 32pp. 4½ x 6⅜. 22560-7 Pa. $1.00

MARMADUKE MULTIPLY'S MERRY METHOD OF MAKING MINOR MATHEMATICIANS. Fellow to Peter Piper, it teaches multiplication table by catchy rhymes and woodcuts. 1841 Munroe & Francis edition. Edited by E.F. Bleiler. 103pp. 4⅝ x 6.
22773-1 Pa. $1.25
20171-6 Clothbd. $3.00

THE NIGHT BEFORE CHRISTMAS, Clement Moore. Full text, and woodcuts from original 1848 book. Also critical, historical material. 19 illustrations. 40pp. 4⅝ x 6. 22797-9 Pa. $1.00

THE KING OF THE GOLDEN RIVER, John Ruskin. Victorian children's classic of three brothers, their attempts to reach the Golden River, what becomes of them. Facsimile of original 1889 edition. 22 illustrations. 56pp. 4⅝ x 6⅜.
20066-3 Pa. $1.25

DREAMS OF THE RAREBIT FIEND, Winsor McCay. Pioneer cartoon strip, unexcelled for beauty, imagination, in 60 full sequences. Incredible technical virtuosity, wonderful visual wit. Historical introduction. 62pp. 8⅜ x 11¼. 21347-1 Pa. $2.50

THE KATZENJAMMER KIDS, Rudolf Dirks. In full color, 14 strips from 1906-7; full of imagination, characteristic humor. Classic of great historical importance. Introduction by August Derleth. 32pp. 9¼ x 12¼. 23005-8 Pa. $2.00

LITTLE ORPHAN ANNIE AND LITTLE ORPHAN ANNIE IN COSMIC CITY, Harold Gray. Two great sequences from the early strips: our curly-haired heroine defends the Warbucks' financial empire and, then, takes on meanie Phineas P. Pinchpenny. Leapin' lizards! 178pp. 6⅛ x 8⅜. 23107-0 Pa. $2.00

WHEN A FELLER NEEDS A FRIEND, Clare Briggs. 122 cartoons by one of the greatest newspaper cartoonists of the early 20th century — about growing up, making a living, family life, daily frustrations and occasional triumphs. 121pp. 8½ x 9½.
23148-8 Pa. $2.50

THE BEST OF GLUYAS WILLIAMS. 100 drawings by one of America's finest cartoonists: The Day a Cake of Ivory Soap Sank at Proctor & Gamble's, At the Life Insurance Agents' Banquet, and many other gems from the 20's and 30's. 118pp. 8⅜ x 11¼. 22737-5 Pa. $2.50

THE BEST DR. THORNDYKE DETECTIVE STORIES, R. Austin Freeman. The Case of Oscar Brodski, The Moabite Cipher, and 5 other favorites featuring the great scientific detective, plus his long-believed-lost first adventure — 31 New Inn — reprinted here for the first time. Edited by E.F. Bleiler. USO 20388-3 Pa. $3.00

BEST "THINKING MACHINE" DETECTIVE STORIES, Jacques Futrelle. The Problem of Cell 13 and 11 other stories about Prof. Augustus S.F.X. Van Dusen, including two "lost" stories. First reprinting of several. Edited by E.F. Bleiler. 241pp.
20537-1 Pa. $3.00

UNCLE SILAS, J. Sheridan LeFanu. Victorian Gothic mystery novel, considered by many best of period, even better than Collins or Dickens. Wonderful psychological terror. Introduction by Frederick Shroyer. 436pp. 21715-9 Pa. $4.00

BEST DR. POGGIOLI DETECTIVE STORIES, T.S. Stribling. 15 best stories from EQMM and The Saint offer new adventures in Mexico, Florida, Tennessee hills as Poggioli unravels mysteries and combats Count Jalacki. 217pp. 23227-1 Pa. $3.00

EIGHT DIME NOVELS, selected with an introduction by E.F. Bleiler. Adventures of Old King Brady, Frank James, Nick Carter, Deadwood Dick, Buffalo Bill, The Steam Man, Frank Merriwell, and Horatio Alger — 1877 to 1905. Important, entertaining popular literature in facsimile reprint, with original covers. 190pp. 9 x 12.
22975-0 Pa. $3.50

ALICE'S ADVENTURES UNDER GROUND, Lewis Carroll. Facsimile of ms. Carroll gave Alice Liddell in 1864. Different in many ways from final Alice. Handlettered, illustrated by Carroll. Introduction by Martin Gardner. 128pp. 21482-6 Pa. $1.50

ALICE IN WONDERLAND COLORING BOOK, Lewis Carroll. Pictures by John Tenniel. Large-size versions of the famous illustrations of Alice, Cheshire Cat, Mad Hatter and all the others, waiting for your crayons. Abridged text. 36 illustrations. 64pp. 8¼ x 11.
22853-3 Pa. $1.50

AVENTURES D'ALICE AU PAYS DES MERVEILLES, Lewis Carroll. Bué's translation of "Alice" into French, supervised by Carroll himself. Novel way to learn language. (No English text.) 42 Tenniel illustrations. 196pp. 22836-3 Pa. $2.50

MYTHS AND FOLK TALES OF IRELAND, Jeremiah Curtin. 11 stories that are Irish versions of European fairy tales and 9 stories from the Fenian cycle — 20 tales of legend and magic that comprise an essential work in the history of folklore. 256pp.
22430-9 Pa. $3.00

EAST O' THE SUN AND WEST O' THE MOON, George W. Dasent. Only full edition of favorite, wonderful Norwegian fairytales — Why the Sea is Salt, Boots and the Troll, etc. — with 77 illustrations by Kittelsen & Werenskiöld. 418pp.
22521-6 Pa. $4.00

PERRAULT'S FAIRY TALES, Charles Perrault and Gustave Doré. Original versions of Cinderella, Sleeping Beauty, Little Red Riding Hood, etc. in best translation, with 34 wonderful illustrations by Gustave Doré. 117pp. 8⅛ x 11. 22311-6 Pa. $2.50

EARLY NEW ENGLAND GRAVESTONE RUBBINGS, Edmund V. Gillon, Jr. 43 photographs, 226 rubbings show heavily symbolic, macabre, sometimes humorous primitive American art. Up to early 19th century. 207pp. 8⅜ x 11¼.
21380-3 Pa. $4.00

L.J.M. DAGUERRE: THE HISTORY OF THE DIORAMA AND THE DAGUERREOTYPE, Helmut and Alison Gernsheim. Definitive account. Early history, life and work of Daguerre; discovery of daguerreotype process; diffusion abroad; other early photography. 124 illustrations. 226pp. 6⅙ x 9¼.
22290-X Pa. $4.00

PHOTOGRAPHY AND THE AMERICAN SCENE, Robert Taft. The basic book on American photography as art, recording form, 1839-1889. Development, influence on society, great photographers, types (portraits, war, frontier, etc.), whatever else needed. Inexhaustible. Illustrated with 322 early photos, daguerreotypes, tintypes, stereo slides, etc. 546pp. 6⅛ x 9¼.
21201-7 Pa. $5.95

PHOTOGRAPHIC SKETCHBOOK OF THE CIVIL WAR, Alexander Gardner. Reproduction of 1866 volume with 100 on-the-field photographs: Manassas, Lincoln on battlefield, slave pens, etc. Introduction by E.F. Bleiler. 224pp. 10¾ x 9.
22731-6 Pa. $5.00

THE MOVIES: A PICTURE QUIZ BOOK, Stanley Appelbaum & Hayward Cirker. Match stars with their movies, name actors and actresses, test your movie skill with 241 stills from 236 great movies, 1902-1959. Indexes of performers and films. 128pp. 8⅜ x 9¼.
20222-4 Pa. $2.50

THE TALKIES, Richard Griffith. Anthology of features, articles from Photoplay, 1928-1940, reproduced complete. Stars, famous movies, technical features, fabulous ads, etc.; Garbo, Chaplin, King Kong, Lubitsch, etc. 4 color plates, scores of illustrations. 327pp. 8⅜ x 11¼.
22762-6 Pa. $6.95

THE MOVIE MUSICAL FROM VITAPHONE TO "42ND STREET," edited by Miles Kreuger. Relive the rise of the movie musical as reported in the pages of Photoplay magazine (1926-1933): every movie review, cast list, ad, and record review; every significant feature article, production still, biography, forecast, and gossip story. Profusely illustrated. 367pp. 8⅜ x 11¼.
23154-2 Pa. $6.95

JOHANN SEBASTIAN BACH, Philipp Spitta. Great classic of biography, musical commentary, with hundreds of pieces analyzed. Also good for Bach's contemporaries. 450 musical examples. Total of 1799pp.
EUK 22278-0, 22279-9 Clothbd., Two vol. set $25.00

BEETHOVEN AND HIS NINE SYMPHONIES, Sir George Grove. Thorough history, analysis, commentary on symphonies and some related pieces. For either beginner or advanced student. 436 musical passages. 407pp.
20334-4 Pa. $4.00

MOZART AND HIS PIANO CONCERTOS, Cuthbert Girdlestone. The only full-length study. Detailed analyses of all 21 concertos, sources; 417 musical examples. 509pp.
21271-8 Pa. $4.50

THE FITZWILLIAM VIRGINAL BOOK, edited by J. Fuller Maitland, W.B. Squire. Famous early 17th century collection of keyboard music, 300 works by Morley, Byrd, Bull, Gibbons, etc. Modern notation. Total of 938pp. 8⅜ x 11.
ECE 21068-5, 21069-3 Pa., Two vol. set $14.00

COMPLETE STRING QUARTETS, Wolfgang A. Mozart. Breitkopf and Härtel edition. All 23 string quartets plus alternate slow movement to K156. Study score. 277pp. 9⅜ x 12¼.
22372-8 Pa. $6.00

COMPLETE SONG CYCLES, Franz Schubert. Complete piano, vocal music of Die Schöne Müllerin, Die Winterreise, Schwanengesang. Also Drinker English singing translations. Breitkopf and Härtel edition. 217pp. 9⅜ x 12¼.
22649-2 Pa. $4.50

THE COMPLETE PRELUDES AND ETUDES FOR PIANOFORTE SOLO, Alexander Scriabin. All the preludes and etudes including many perfectly spun miniatures. Edited by K.N. Igumnov and Y.I. Mil'shteyn. 250pp. 9 x 12.
22919-X Pa. $5.00

TRISTAN UND ISOLDE, Richard Wagner. Full orchestral score with complete instrumentation. Do not confuse with piano reduction. Commentary by Felix Mottl, great Wagnerian conductor and scholar. Study score. 655pp. 8⅛ x 11.
22915-7 Pa. $10.00

FAVORITE SONGS OF THE NINETIES, ed. Robert Fremont. Full reproduction, including covers, of 88 favorites: Ta-Ra-Ra-Boom-De-Aye, The Band Played On, Bird in a Gilded Cage, Under the Bamboo Tree, After the Ball, etc. 401pp. 9 x 12.
EBE 21536-9 Pa. $6.95

SOUSA'S GREAT MARCHES IN PIANO TRANSCRIPTION: ORIGINAL SHEET MUSIC OF 23 WORKS, John Philip Sousa. Selected by Lester S. Levy. Playing edition includes: The Stars and Stripes Forever, The Thunderer, The Gladiator, King Cotton, Washington Post, much more. 24 illustrations. 111pp. 9 x 12.
USO 23132-1 Pa. $3.50

CLASSIC PIANO RAGS, selected with an introduction by Rudi Blesh. Best ragtime music (1897-1922) by Scott Joplin, James Scott, Joseph F. Lamb, Tom Turpin, 9 others. Printed from best original sheet music, plus covers. 364pp. 9 x 12.
EBE 20469-3 Pa. $6.95

ANALYSIS OF CHINESE CHARACTERS, C.D. Wilder, J.H. Ingram. 1000 most important characters analyzed according to primitives, phonetics, historical development. Traditional method offers mnemonic aid to beginner, intermediate student of Chinese, Japanese. 365pp.
23045-7 Pa. $4.00

MODERN CHINESE: A BASIC COURSE, Faculty of Peking University. Self study, classroom course in modern Mandarin. Records contain phonetics, vocabulary, sentences, lessons. 249 page book contains all recorded text, translations, grammar, vocabulary, exercises. Best course on market. 3 12" 33⅓ monaural records, book, album.
98832-5 Set $12.50

MANUAL OF THE TREES OF NORTH AMERICA, Charles S. Sargent. The basic survey of every native tree and tree-like shrub, 717 species in all. Extremely full descriptions, information on habitat, growth, locales, economics, etc. Necessary to every serious tree lover. Over 100 finding keys. 783 illustrations. Total of 986pp.
20277-1, 20278-X Pa., Two vol. set $8.00

BIRDS OF THE NEW YORK AREA, John Bull. Indispensable guide to more than 400 species within a hundred-mile radius of Manhattan. Information on range, status, breeding, migration, distribution trends, etc. Foreword by Roger Tory Peterson. 17 drawings; maps. 540pp.
23222-0 Pa. $6.00

THE SEA-BEACH AT EBB-TIDE, Augusta Foote Arnold. Identify hundreds of marine plants and animals: algae, seaweeds, squids, crabs, corals, etc. Descriptions cover food, life cycle, size, shape, habitat. Over 600 drawings. 490pp.
21949-6 Pa. $5.00

THE MOTH BOOK, William J. Holland. Identify more than 2,000 moths of North America. General information, precise species descriptions. 623 illustrations plus 48 color plates show almost all species, full size. 1968 edition. Still the basic book. Total of 551pp. 6½ x 9¼.
21948-8 Pa. $6.00

AN INTRODUCTION TO THE REPTILES AND AMPHIBIANS OF THE UNITED STATES, Percy A. Morris. All lizards, crocodiles, turtles, snakes, toads, frogs; life history, identification, habits, suitability as pets, etc. Non-technical, but sound and broad. 130 photos. 253pp.
22982-3 Pa. $3.00

OLD NEW YORK IN EARLY PHOTOGRAPHS, edited by Mary Black. Your only chance to see New York City as it was 1853-1906, through 196 wonderful photographs from N.Y. Historical Society. Great Blizzard, Lincoln's funeral procession, great buildings. 228pp. 9 x 12.
22907-6 Pa. $6.00

THE AMERICAN REVOLUTION, A PICTURE SOURCEBOOK, John Grafton. Wonderful Bicentennial picture source, with 411 illustrations (contemporary and 19th century) showing battles, personalities, maps, events, flags, posters, soldier's life, ships, etc. all captioned and explained. A wonderful browsing book, supplement to other historical reading. 160pp. 9 x 12.
23226-3 Pa. $4.00

PERSONAL NARRATIVE OF A PILGRIMAGE TO AL-MADINAH AND MECCAH, Richard Burton. Great travel classic by remarkably colorful personality. Burton, disguised as a Moroccan, visited sacred shrines of Islam, narrowly escaping death. Wonderful observations of Islamic life, customs, personalities. 47 illustrations. Total of 959pp.
21217-3, 21218-1 Pa., Two vol. set $10.00

INCIDENTS OF TRAVEL IN CENTRAL AMERICA, CHIAPAS, AND YUCATAN, John L. Stephens. Almost single-handed discovery of Maya culture; exploration of ruined cities, monuments, temples; customs of Indians. 115 drawings. 892pp.
22404-X, 22405-8 Pa., Two vol. set $8.00

CONSTRUCTION OF AMERICAN FURNITURE TREASURES, Lester Margon. 344 detail drawings, complete text on constructing exact reproductions of 38 early American masterpieces: Hepplewhite sideboard, Duncan Phyfe drop-leaf table, mantel clock, gate-leg dining table, Pa. German cupboard, more. 38 plates. 54 photographs. 168pp. 8⅜ x 11¼.   23056-2 Pa. $4.00

JEWELRY MAKING AND DESIGN, Augustus F. Rose, Antonio Cirino. Professional secrets revealed in thorough, practical guide: tools, materials, processes; rings, brooches, chains, cast pieces, enamelling, setting stones, etc. Do not confuse with skimpy introductions: beginner can use, professional can learn from it. Over 200 illustrations. 306pp.   21750-7 Pa. $3.00

METALWORK AND ENAMELLING, Herbert Maryon. Generally conceded best all-around book. Countless trade secrets: materials, tools, soldering, filigree, setting, inlay, niello, repoussé, casting, polishing, etc. For beginner or expert. Author was foremost British expert. 330 illustrations. 335pp.   22702-2 Pa. $3.50

WEAVING WITH FOOT-POWER LOOMS, Edward F. Worst. Setting up a loom, beginning to weave, constructing equipment, using dyes, more, plus over 285 drafts of traditional patterns including Colonial and Swedish weaves. More than 200 other figures. For beginning and advanced. 275pp. 8¾ x 6⅜.   23064-3 Pa. $4.00

WEAVING A NAVAJO BLANKET, Gladys A. Reichard. Foremost anthropologist studied under Navajo women, reveals every step in process from wool, dyeing, spinning, setting up loom, designing, weaving. Much history, symbolism. With this book you could make one yourself. 97 illustrations. 222pp.   22992-0 Pa. $3.00

NATURAL DYES AND HOME DYEING, Rita J. Adrosko. Use natural ingredients: bark, flowers, leaves, lichens, insects etc. Over 135 specific recipes from historical sources for cotton, wool, other fabrics. Genuine premodern handicrafts. 12 illustrations. 160pp.   22688-3 Pa. $2.00

THE HAND DECORATION OF FABRICS, Francis J. Kafka. Outstanding, profusely illustrated guide to stenciling, batik, block printing, tie dyeing, freehand painting, silk screen printing, and novelty decoration. 356 illustrations. 198pp. 6 x 9.
21401-X Pa. $3.00

THOMAS NAST: CARTOONS AND ILLUSTRATIONS, with text by Thomas Nast St. Hill. Father of American political cartooning. Cartoons that destroyed Tweed Ring; inflation, free love, church and state; original Republican elephant and Democratic donkey; Santa Claus; more. 117 illustrations. 146pp. 9 x 12.
22983-1 Pa. $4.00
23067-8 Clothbd. $8.50

FREDERIC REMINGTON: 173 DRAWINGS AND ILLUSTRATIONS. Most famous of the Western artists, most responsible for our myths about the American West in its untamed days. Complete reprinting of *Drawings of Frederic Remington* (1897), plus other selections. 4 additional drawings in color on covers. 140pp. 9 x 12.
20714-5 Pa. $3.95

How to Solve Chess Problems, Kenneth S. Howard. Practical suggestions on problem solving for very beginners. 58 two-move problems, 46 3-movers, 8 4-movers for practice, plus hints. 171pp. 20748-X Pa. $2.00

A Guide to Fairy Chess, Anthony Dickins. 3-D chess, 4-D chess, chess on a cylindrical board, reflecting pieces that bounce off edges, cooperative chess, retrograde chess, maximummers, much more. Most based on work of great Dawson. Full handbook, 100 problems. 66pp. 7⅞ x 10¾. 22687-5 Pa. $2.00

Win at Backgammon, Millard Hopper. Best opening moves, running game, blocking game, back game, tables of odds, etc. Hopper makes the game clear enough for anyone to play, and win. 43 diagrams. 111pp. 22894-0 Pa. $1.50

Bidding a Bridge Hand, Terence Reese. Master player "thinks out loud" the binding of 75 hands that defy point count systems. Organized by bidding problem—no-fit situations, overbidding, underbidding, cueing your defense, etc. 254pp. EBE 22830-4 Pa. $2.50

The Precision Bidding System in Bridge, C.C. Wei, edited by Alan Truscott. Inventor of precision bidding presents average hands and hands from actual play, including games from 1969 Bermuda Bowl where system emerged. 114 exercises. 116pp. 21171-1 Pa. $1.75

Learn Magic, Henry Hay. 20 simple, easy-to-follow lessons on magic for the new magician: illusions, card tricks, silks, sleights of hand, coin manipulations, escapes, and more —all with a minimum amount of equipment. Final chapter explains the great stage illusions. 92 illustrations. 285pp. 21238-6 Pa. $2.95

The New Magician's Manual, Walter B. Gibson. Step-by-step instructions and clear illustrations guide the novice in mastering 36 tricks; much equipment supplied on 16 pages of cut-out materials. 36 additional tricks. 64 illustrations. 159pp. 6⅝ x 10. 23113-5 Pa. $3.00

Professional Magic for Amateurs, Walter B. Gibson. 50 easy, effective tricks used by professionals —cards, string, tumblers, handkerchiefs, mental magic, etc. 63 illustrations. 223pp. 23012-0 Pa. $2.50

Card Manipulations, Jean Hugard. Very rich collection of manipulations; has taught thousands of fine magicians tricks that are really workable, eye-catching. Easily followed, serious work. Over 200 illustrations. 163pp. 20539-8 Pa. $2.00

Abbott's Encyclopedia of Rope Tricks for Magicians, Stewart James. Complete reference book for amateur and professional magicians containing more than 150 tricks involving knots, penetrations, cut and restored rope, etc. 510 illustrations. Reprint of 3rd edition. 400pp. 23206-9 Pa. $3.50

The Secrets of Houdini, J.C. Cannell. Classic study of Houdini's incredible magic, exposing closely-kept professional secrets and revealing, in general terms, the whole art of stage magic. 67 illustrations. 279pp. 22913-0 Pa. $2.50

CATALOGUE OF DOVER BOOKS

THE MAGIC MOVING PICTURE BOOK, Bliss, Sands & Co. The pictures in this book move! Volcanoes erupt, a house burns, a serpentine dancer wiggles her way through a number. By using a specially ruled acetate screen provided, you can obtain these and 15 other startling effects. Originally "The Motograph Moving Picture Book." 32pp. 8¼ x 11. 23224-7 Pa. $1.75

STRING FIGURES AND HOW TO MAKE THEM, Caroline F. Jayne. Fullest, clearest instructions on string figures from around world: Eskimo, Navajo, Lapp, Europe, more. Cats cradle, moving spear, lightning, stars. Introduction by A.C. Haddon. 950 illustrations. 407pp. 20152-X Pa. $3.00

PAPER FOLDING FOR BEGINNERS, William D. Murray and Francis J. Rigney. Clearest book on market for making origami sail boats, roosters, frogs that move legs, cups, bonbon boxes. 40 projects. More than 275 illustrations. Photographs. 94pp. 20713-7 Pa. $1.25

INDIAN SIGN LANGUAGE, William Tomkins. Over 525 signs developed by Sioux, Blackfoot, Cheyenne, Arapahoe and other tribes. Written instructions and diagrams: how to make words, construct sentences. Also 290 pictographs of Sioux and Ojibway tribes. 111pp. 6⅛ x 9¼. 22029-X Pa. $1.50

BOOMERANGS: HOW TO MAKE AND THROW THEM, Bernard S. Mason. Easy to make and throw, dozens of designs: cross-stick, pinwheel, boomabird, tumblestick, Australian curved stick boomerang. Complete throwing instructions. All safe. 99pp. 23028-7 Pa. $1.50

25 KITES THAT FLY, Leslie Hunt. Full, easy to follow instructions for kites made from inexpensive materials. Many novelties. Reeling, raising, designing your own. 70 illustrations. 110pp. 22550-X Pa. $1.25

TRICKS AND GAMES ON THE POOL TABLE, Fred Herrmann. 79 tricks and games, some solitaires, some for 2 or more players, some competitive; mystifying shots and throws, unusual carom, tricks involving cork, coins, a hat, more. 77 figures. 95pp. 21814-7 Pa. $1.25

WOODCRAFT AND CAMPING, Bernard S. Mason. How to make a quick emergency shelter, select woods that will burn immediately, make do with limited supplies, etc. Also making many things out of wood, rawhide, bark, at camp. Formerly titled Woodcraft. 295 illustrations. 580pp. 21951-8 Pa. $4.00

AN INTRODUCTION TO CHESS MOVES AND TACTICS SIMPLY EXPLAINED, Leonard Barden. Informal intermediate introduction: reasons for moves, tactics, openings, traps, positional play, endgame. Isolates patterns. 102pp. USO 21210-6 Pa. $1.35

LASKER'S MANUAL OF CHESS, Dr. Emanuel Lasker. Great world champion offers very thorough coverage of all aspects of chess. Combinations, position play, openings, endgame, aesthetics of chess, philosophy of struggle, much more. Filled with analyzed games. 390pp. 20640-8 Pa. $3.50

SLEEPING BEAUTY, illustrated by Arthur Rackham. Perhaps the fullest, most delightful version ever, told by C.S. Evans. Rackham's best work. 49 illustrations. 110pp. 7⁷/₈ x 10¾. 22756-1 Pa. $2.00

THE WONDERFUL WIZARD OF OZ, L. Frank Baum. Facsimile in full color of America's finest children's classic. Introduction by Martin Gardner. 143 illustrations by W.W. Denslow. 267pp. 20691-2 Pa. $2.50

GOOPS AND HOW TO BE THEM, Gelett Burgess. Classic tongue-in-cheek masquerading as etiquette book. 87 verses, 170 cartoons as Goops demonstrate virtues of table manners, neatness, courtesy, more. 88pp. 6½ x 9¼.
22233-0 Pa. $1.50

THE BROWNIES, THEIR BOOK, Palmer Cox. Small as mice, cunning as foxes, exuberant, mischievous, Brownies go to zoo, toy shop, seashore, circus, more. 24 verse adventures. 266 illustrations. 144pp. 6⁵/₈ x 9¼. 21265-3 Pa. $1.75

BILLY WHISKERS: THE AUTOBIOGRAPHY OF A GOAT, Frances Trego Montgomery. Escapades of that rambunctious goat. Favorite from turn of the century America. 24 illustrations. 259pp. 22345-0 Pa. $2.75

THE ROCKET BOOK, Peter Newell. Fritz, janitor's kid, sets off rocket in basement of apartment house; an ingenious hole punched through every page traces course of rocket. 22 duotone drawings, verses. 48pp. 6⁷/₈ x 8³/₈. 22044-3 Pa. $1.50

PECK'S BAD BOY AND HIS PA, George W. Peck. Complete double-volume of great American childhood classic. Hennery's ingenious pranks against outraged pomposity of pa and the grocery man. 97 illustrations. Introduction by E.F. Bleiler. 347pp. 20497-9 Pa. $2.50

THE TALE OF PETER RABBIT, Beatrix Potter. The inimitable Peter's terrifying adventure in Mr. McGregor's garden, with all 27 wonderful, full-color Potter illustrations. 55pp. 4¼ x 5½. USO 22827-4 Pa. $1.00

THE TALE OF MRS. TIGGY-WINKLE, Beatrix Potter. Your child will love this story about a very special hedgehog and all 27 wonderful, full-color Potter illustrations. 57pp. 4¼ x 5½. USO 20546-0 Pa. $1.00

THE TALE OF BENJAMIN BUNNY, Beatrix Potter. Peter Rabbit's cousin coaxes him back into Mr. McGregor's garden for a whole new set of adventures. A favorite with children. All 27 full-color illustrations. 59pp. 4¼ x 5½.
USO 21102-9 Pa. $1.00

THE MERRY ADVENTURES OF ROBIN HOOD, Howard Pyle. Facsimile of original (1883) edition, finest modern version of English outlaw's adventures. 23 illustrations by Pyle. 296pp. 6½ x 9¼. 22043-5 Pa. $2.75

TWO LITTLE SAVAGES, Ernest Thompson Seton. Adventures of two boys who lived as Indians; explaining Indian ways, woodlore, pioneer methods. 293 illustrations. 286pp. 20985-7 Pa. $3.00

HOUDINI ON MAGIC, Harold Houdini. Edited by Walter Gibson, Morris N. Young. How he escaped; exposés of fake spiritualists; instructions for eye-catching tricks; other fascinating material by and about greatest magician. 155 illustrations. 280pp. 20384-0 Pa. $2.50

HANDBOOK OF THE NUTRITIONAL CONTENTS OF FOOD, U.S. Dept. of Agriculture. Largest, most detailed source of food nutrition information ever prepared. Two mammoth tables: one measuring nutrients in 100 grams of edible portion; the other, in edible portion of 1 pound as purchased. Originally titled Composition of Foods. 190pp. 9 x 12. 21342-0 Pa. $4.00

COMPLETE GUIDE TO HOME CANNING, PRESERVING AND FREEZING, U.S. Dept. of Agriculture. Seven basic manuals with full instructions for jams and jellies; pickles and relishes; canning fruits, vegetables, meat; freezing anything. Really good recipes, exact instructions for optimal results. Save a fortune in food. 156 illustrations. 214pp. 6⅛ x 9¼. 22911-4 Pa. $2.50

THE BREAD TRAY, Louis P. De Gouy. Nearly every bread the cook could buy or make: bread sticks of Italy, fruit breads of Greece, glazed rolls of Vienna, everything from corn pone to croissants. Over 500 recipes altogether. including buns, rolls, muffins, scones, and more. 463pp. 23000-7 Pa. $3.50

CREATIVE HAMBURGER COOKERY, Louis P. De Gouy. 182 unusual recipes for casseroles, meat loaves and hamburgers that turn inexpensive ground meat into memorable main dishes: Arizona chili burgers, burger tamale pie, burger stew, burger corn loaf, burger wine loaf, and more. 120pp. 23001-5 Pa. $1.75

LONG ISLAND SEAFOOD COOKBOOK, J. George Frederick and Jean Joyce. Probably the best American seafood cookbook. Hundreds of recipes. 40 gourmet sauces, 123 recipes using oysters alone! All varieties of fish and seafood amply represented. 324pp. 22677-8 Pa. $3.00

THE EPICUREAN: A COMPLETE TREATISE OF ANALYTICAL AND PRACTICAL STUDIES IN THE CULINARY ART, Charles Ranhofer. Great modern classic. 3,500 recipes from master chef of Delmonico's, turn-of-the-century America's best restaurant. Also explained, many techniques known only to professional chefs. 775 illustrations. 1183pp. 6⅝ x 10. 22680-8 Clothbd. $17.50

THE AMERICAN WINE COOK BOOK, Ted Hatch. Over 700 recipes: old favorites livened up with wine plus many more: Czech fish soup, quince soup, sauce Perigueux, shrimp shortcake, filets Stroganoff, cordon bleu goulash, jambonneau, wine fruit cake, more. 314pp. 22796-0 Pa. $2.50

DELICIOUS VEGETARIAN COOKING, Ivan Baker. Close to 500 delicious and varied recipes: soups, main course dishes (pea, bean, lentil, cheese, vegetable, pasta, and egg dishes), savories, stews, whole-wheat breads and cakes, more. 168pp. USO 22834-7 Pa. $1.75

COOKIES FROM MANY LANDS, Josephine Perry. Crullers, oatmeal cookies, chaux au chocolate, English tea cakes, mandel kuchen, Sacher torte, Danish puff pastry, Swedish cookies — a mouth-watering collection of 223 recipes. 157pp.

22832-0 Pa. $2.00

ROSE RECIPES, Eleanour S. Rohde. How to make sauces, jellies, tarts, salads, pot-pourris, sweet bags, pomanders, perfumes from garden roses; all exact recipes. Century old favorites. 95pp.

22957-2 Pa. $1.25

"OSCAR" OF THE WALDORF'S COOKBOOK, Oscar Tschirky. Famous American chef reveals 3455 recipes that made Waldorf great; cream of French, German, American cooking, in all categories. Full instructions, easy home use. 1896 edition. 907pp. 6⅝ x 9⅜.

20790-0 Clothbd. $15.00

JAMS AND JELLIES, May Byron. Over 500 old-time recipes for delicious jams, jellies, marmalades, preserves, and many other items. Probably the largest jam and jelly book in print. Originally titled May Byron's Jam Book. 276pp.

USO 23130-5 Pa. $3.00

MUSHROOM RECIPES, André L. Simon. 110 recipes for everyday and special cooking. Champignons a la grecque, sole bonne femme, chicken liver croustades, more; 9 basic sauces, 13 ways of cooking mushrooms. 54pp.

USO 20913-X Pa. $1.25

FAVORITE SWEDISH RECIPES, edited by Sam Widenfelt. Prepared in Sweden, offers wonderful, clearly explained Swedish dishes: appetizers, meats, pastry and cookies, other categories. Suitable for American kitchen. 90 photos. 157pp.

23156-9 Pa. $2.00

THE BUCKEYE COOKBOOK, Buckeye Publishing Company. Over 1,000 easy-to-follow, traditional recipes from the American Midwest: bread (100 recipes alone), meat, game, jam, candy, cake, ice cream, and many other categories of cooking. 64 illustrations. From 1883 enlarged edition. 416pp. 23218-2 Pa. $4.00

TWENTY-TWO AUTHENTIC BANQUETS FROM INDIA, Robert H. Christie. Complete, easy-to-do recipes for almost 200 authentic Indian dishes assembled in 22 banquets. Arranged by region. Selected from Banquets of the Nations. 192pp.

23200-X Pa. $2.50

Prices subject to change without notice.
Available at your book dealer or write for free catalogue to Dept. GI, Dover Publications, Inc., 180 Varick St., N.Y., N.Y. 10014. Dover publishes more than 150 books each year on science, elementary and advanced mathematics, biology, music, art, literary history, social sciences and other areas.